Quilt It
with Wool

Quilt It with Wool

Nathalie Mornu

Projects Stitched on Tartans, Tweeds & Other Toasty Fabrics

LARK BOOKS

A Division of Sterling Publishing Co., Inc.
New York / London

Art Director: **Kristi Pfeffer**
Photographer: **Sandra Stambaugh**
Illustrator: **Olivier Rollin**
Production: **Kay Stafford**
Cover Designer: **Lana Lê**

Library of Congress Cataloging-in-Publication Data

Quilt it with wool : projects stitched on tartans, tweeds & other toasty fabrics. -- 1st ed.
   p. cm.
 Includes index.
 ISBN 978-1-60059-389-5 (pb-pbk. : alk. paper)
 1. Machine quilting--Patterns. 2. Wool fabrics. I. Lark Books.
 TT835.Q487 2010
 746.46'041--dc22

                                    2008054381

10 9 8 7 6 5 4 3 2 1

First Edition

Published by Lark Books, A Division of
Sterling Publishing Co., Inc.
387 Park Avenue South, New York, NY 10016

Distributed in Canada by Sterling Publishing,
c/o Canadian Manda Group, 165 Dufferin Street
Toronto, Ontario, Canada M6K 3H6

Distributed in the United Kingdom by GMC Distribution Services,
Castle Place, 166 High Street, Lewes, East Sussex, England BN7 1XU

Distributed in Australia by Capricorn Link (Australia) Pty Ltd.,
P.O. Box 704, Windsor, NSW 2756 Australia

If you have questions or comments about this book, please contact:
Lark Books
67 Broadway
Asheville, NC 28801
828-253-0467

Manufactured in China

ISBN 13: 978-1-60059-389-5

For information about custom editions, special sales, or premium and corporate purchases, please contact the Sterling Special Sales Department at 800-805-5489 or specialsales@sterlingpub.com.

Contents

Why Wool? *page 8*

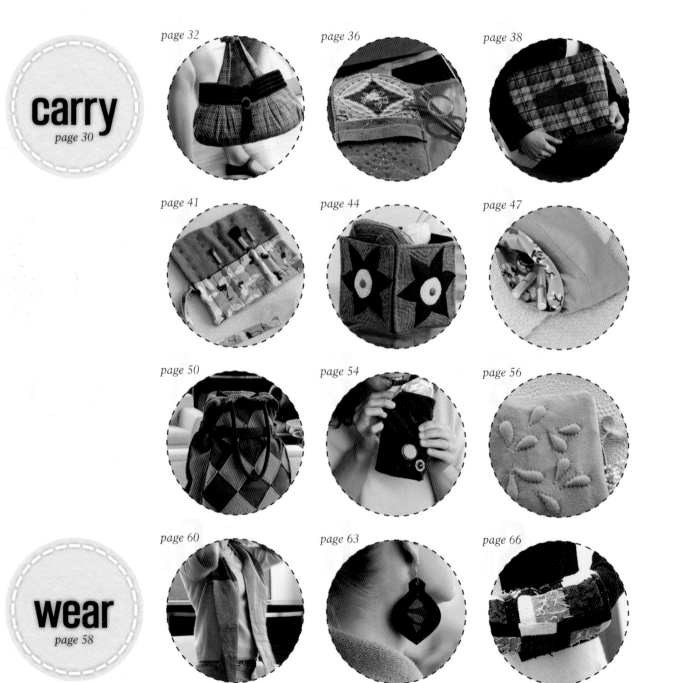

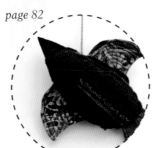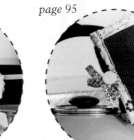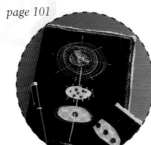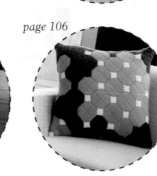

Ready to take your quilting to the next level? It's time to throw wool fabrics into the mix. They've got texture, color, sophistication. Chameleon-like, raw wool can be turned into all types of cloth—and whether they're heavy or lightweight, smooth or textured, soft or stiff, these fabrics always look rich, crisp, and appealing.

You might not immediately think to quilt with wool, but it's clear why this warm, fuzzy material is an emerging trend with quilters, sewers, and crafters. Its extra weight makes any project especially cozy; wools come in great patterns and solids in lustrous, divine hues; you can sew them to cottons, silks, and other fabrics without a bit of fuss; and, oh, their tactile appeal! Just imagine the contrast of a fuzzy boiled wool quilt bound with cool satin, or a smooth wool suiting embellished with nubby wool appliqués.

Although this book includes two snuggly quilts, our designers have gone well beyond bed coverings. In the chapter called Carry, you'll find striking bags—some feature spot quilting—as well as an assortment of containers for storing anything, from make-up brushes to laptops. The section named Wear contains all kinds of stuff to put on. There's a flirty '50s-styled capelet with overall quilting and a tartan lining, and a scarf made of the latest, hottest thing in wools: overdyed fabric. Look for the unexpected, too—check out the quilted earrings on page 63 and the muff on page 66.

In Live, you'll find
toss pillows (the quilting
on the cushion on page 85 was
inspired by the Japanese sashiko
technique) and the honeycomb-inspired
table runner on our cover, as well as surprising items
like a draft stopper and an adorable padded cozy to
wrap around the handle of a tea kettle.

Throughout the book, you'll come across techniques as
diverse as appliqué, stamping, and the semi-forgotten
trapunto, and you'll discover clever ideas for embellish-
ing your projects. Just glance at the mobile on page 82,
for example. The birdies would be sweet even without
adornment, but isn't the ribbon and trim added to their
tummies too, too charming? Some projects start with
fabric off a bolt, others re-purpose old garments, and
still others are made from high-quality craft felt or
sweaters you felt yourself. Almost all mix wool fabrics
with other cloth types.

Wool has been the fiber of choice of countless cultures
for thousands of years. You sensible types can already
sing its praises: entirely renewable and natural,
water-repellent, wrinkle- and fade-resistant, warm in
cold temperatures and cool in warm weather. (Some
wools are even machine washable!) So flip through these
pages to admire all the great quilted projects you can
make. Now pick one, gather some wool, and take your
quilting up a notch. You'll wonder why you didn't start
quilting with wool sooner.

Quilting Components

Regardless of whether you're making an actual quilt, a home accessory, something to wear, or a pretty purse, the components that make up every quilted piece are the same. Quilting is the combination of three main elements—the top, the backing, and the batting. You stack these three elements together, with the batting in the middle, to make the *quilt sandwich*. Then you attach the layers together with either decorative stitching across the broad areas of the sandwich—this is quilting—or knots. Finally, you catch the perimeters of the sandwich in binding if you're making a quilt, or in a seam if you're making a three-dimensional object. *Voilà*. It's such a straightforward sewing process that you can reserve all your creative juices for choosing and arranging your wool stash.

Top and Backing

The top of any quilted item is usually the decorative focus. It can be simple or intricate. It can be blocks or shapes of fabric joined together, or it can be a single fabric embellished with appliqués or decorative stitching. It's like a piece of art—how cool is that?

The back of the quilt is the supporting fabric. It's usually less elaborate, although there's no reason you can't make it as decorative as the top. If you've pieced the top of the quilt, there's a chance that piece might be larger than the fabric you're using for the backing. No problem. Simply join multiple pieces of backing fabric to create a single piece at least 4 inches (10.2 cm) wider and longer than the quilt top. In stores, you may spot fabrics made specifically for quilt backings that are 90 inches or 108 inches (229 or 274.5 cm) wide—wide enough to back most quilts without piecing.

Even though they start as separate units, the fabrics for the top and the backing become one, so it's important that they be compatible with each other and with the function of the quilt. You can use almost all types of fabrics (page 12) as long as they're of similar weight and have the same laundering and care requirements. Avoid using a heavy or bulky quilt top fabric with a lightweight backing and vice versa. And if the quilt top can be machine washed, you most certainly want the backing to be machine washable. All machine-washable fabrics should be prewashed before you cut them or begin quilting (page 23).

Quilt Batting

Batting is that mysterious middle layer that you can't see, but you know exists because it adds more weight, warmth, and thickness to the quilt. There are many different types from which to choose, so a little knowledge about fiber content, loft, size, and stitching ease will help make the choice easier.

Batting is made from a variety of fibers, such as cotton, cotton/polyester, polyester, wool, silk, bamboo, and alpaca. Cotton, polyester, and cotton/polyester are the most widely used and the easiest to find, although wool batting is a favorite among quilters. Be sure to make note of the care requirements for whichever batting you choose and launder the quilt accordingly; some battings need to be prewashed.

- Natural fiber battings—cotton, wool, and silk—tend to produce a flatter look. They're particularly suited to machine quilting. Synthetic fiber batting (polyester and cotton/polyester) creates a puffier appearance and is perfect for hand stitching and knotting, although the low-loft synthetic battings are also suitable for machine stitching.
- Cotton batting is most suitable for warm-weather use. It's a popular choice because it supports machine stitches so they're even and visible on the exterior.
- Polyester batting is lightweight and the least expensive option; it compacts well and adds a puffy feeling to a quilt. It's ideal for hand stitching.
- Cotton/polyester blend battings are puffier than cotton batting, but still easy to stitch evenly either by hand or by machine. They combine the benefits of cotton with the loftiness of polyester.
- Wool batting is warm and moisture absorbent, and it produces flatter-looking quilting. It's perfect for decorative machine stitching.

Choosing Materials

Loft describes the thickness of batting. Typically, low-loft battings are most suitable for machine-stitched quilting because they maneuver more easily through the sewing machine. High-loft batting is difficult to machine stitch, so it works best for hand-tied quilts. Experiment with different lofts to find the best one for each project.

Some battings, particularly cotton, slip or move during stitching, so they require smaller stitches to ensure even stitching and lump-free quilting. Most battings are labeled with a recommended minimum distance between stitches to prevent any migration of the batting.

Batting is sold in premeasured packages as well as by the yard. If your quilt top is larger than your batting, simply hand sew pieces of batting together so they extend 2 to 4 inches (5.1 to 10.2 cm) beyond all the edges of the quilt top. When sold by the yard, batting goods can be 45 inches (1.1 m), 90 inches (2.3 m), or 120 inches (3 m) wide.

Since you're putting a lot of time and effort into a project, buy the best-quality stuff you can afford. Check the fabric you're considering for color consistency and stability. Crush a corner of the fabric with your hand and see whether it bounces back to its original shape without distorting. Hold it up to the light and look for an even weave and a balance of the lengthwise and crosswise threads. Make sure it feels good and looks like it'll hold up over time.

Wool is resistant to flames. That's why sheep aren't worried about sitting around bonfires making s'mores.

have a smoother surface because they're made of longer fibers that are combed and straightened before spinning. They often have gloss or shine to their surfaces, and are lighter weight than woolens. The following is a list of suggested wool fabrics, but also consider taking apart an old wool coat or cut up a blanket to repurpose the yardage.

Boiled wool is a soft, compact, knit wool that's been shrunk and felted. It's a favorite coat and jacket fabric and very suited to quilt making.

Bouclé has loops or curls on one or both sides. It can be light- or heavyweight and soft or crisp. It's very versatile and often used in dresses, suits, and jackets.

Camel's hair is a wool-like hair fiber from—duh—the camel. It's soft and lustrous and ranges in color from light tan to dark brown.

Cashmere is a very soft fiber that comes from the hair of the Kashmir goat. Cut up an old cashmere sweater and make yourself a luxurious little head pillow.

Crepe is similar to suiting, but with a matte, crinkled surface that's usually created by weaving hard-twist yarns.

Double cloth is reversible, so that each side might differ (or not) in weave, color, yarn, and pattern. Some double cloth can actually be cut apart into two separate layers.

Wool Fabrics

The first step in making wool fabrics involves gathering fleece from sheep or lambs, or from Angora rabbits, alpaca, camels, and other animals, too. Though you can feel free to shear your favorite sheep, it's far simpler to gather your wool fabrics from a fabric store. (Besides, this book doesn't explain how to card, spin, or weave.)

For the projects in this book, you don't have to start with a big piece of fabric; you can make quilt block units from scraps of repurposed fabric. You can even recycle old sweaters, jackets, blankets, scarves, and just about anything else in your "I-dunno-what-to-do-with-this-but-it's-too-cool-to-throw-away" stash. Whether you purchase or repurpose your fabric, make note of the care requirements on the end of the fabric bolt or the care labels on the garments.

There are two basic types of wool fabrics, both suitable choices for quilt making. *Woolens* are made from loosely spun short fibers, so they tend to be soft with a fuzzy texture and have little or no sheen. Worsteds

Double-face coating

Double cloth is reversible.

Wool can absorb up to 30% of its weight in moisture. Scientists are currently experimenting with using low-grade wool to clean up hazardous spills.

Fashion fabrics include the woolens and worsted wools that are available in a wide array of weights, weaves, and patterns. Some popular fashion fabrics that quilt beautifully include **challis**, which has a printed or woven pattern; **gabardine**, which has a high sheen; **tartan**, that highly recognizable plaid fabric; and **jersey**, a knit wool fabric. Other popular and perfectly suitable wool fabrics include **herringbone** (a chevron pattern), **glen plaid** (a small, even check design), **houndstooth** (a four-pointed star check pattern), and **jacquard** (which includes any number of highly complex woven patterns).

Felt is not a woven fabric; instead, it's a mat of fibers bonded together through the application of heat, moisture, and pressure. It comes in many different weights and colors. Wool felt has a more substantial feel to it than the cheap synthetic felts you'll find in craft stores.

If you have an old sweater or a piece of knitted wool that isn't quite dense or strong enough to use as a fabric, you can turn it into felt by compressing the fibers. It's as easy as tossing it into a washing machine. You've probably already felted a wool sweater by accident, in which case you know what to do! (But in case you want instructions on felting, see page 20.)

Flannel is a soft, often lightweight fabric that's been napped to create a fuzzy surface on one or both sides. Flannel is perfect for baby quilts and other lightweight blankets.

Melton is a dense fabric with a short **nap** (which gives a fabric different shades from different angles). It's not glossy, but it's very durable and is often used to make coats, jackets, and blankets.

Merino is one of the softest wools, although it's not as soft as cashmere.

Mohair is made with the long, lustrous fibers of the Angora goat. It's very strong and somewhat spongy and is often blended with other wools to make jackets and scarves.

Wool crepe

Be on the lookout for unusual fabrics like this knit with a jacquard pattern.

This luxurious wool flannel is made of camel hair.

A wool flannel in a tartan pattern.

Felt made from 100% wool feels more substantial than the synthetic felts sold in craft stores.

Fluffy mohair in a
mouth-watering shade

Melton is a
coat-weight
fabric.

Suiting comes in not only
gray, but a variety of base
shades, with different colors
and patterns of stripes.

Tweed fabrics

Overdyed wool is any wool that's been dyed with several different colors of dye (from the same family), one at a time, for a subtle saturation of deep, rich colors. It's gorgeous. Want proof? Admire the scarf on page 60.

Recycled or repurposed wools are those that you take from an existing garment or existing item. Many of the projects in this book contain repurposed fabric; check out the hot water bottle cozy on page 110, for example, which is made from a snazzy old suit. You can obtain substantial pieces of fabric when you cut apart an old coat or an oversized sweater. Just cut the items along the seams and throw the strips of seams away. If the wool ravels, run a zigzag stitch along the cut edges. Use the cut-apart item just as you would fabric yardage.

Suiting refers to a variety of worsted wools that are used to make suits. They're medium- to heavyweight with a smooth surface and are easy to work with. Suiting is a fairly generic term that includes many weaves, textures, and fibers. The most common suiting has a gray base color with different color striped patterns; however, you'll also find other base colors, such as brown and black.

Tweed is a medium- to heavyweight woolen with a textured hand and mottled color due to the combination of different color yarns. It's typically used to make suits and coats. **Donegal tweed** is known for its thick slubs of colored yarns. **Harris tweed**, on the other hand, has a very soft feel.

Drawn and Quartered

Typically, if you purchase a 1/4 yard (22.8 cm) of fabric, you'll get a piece 9 inches (23 cm) long by the width of the fabric, which isn't always wide enough for quilt shapes. So some quilt shops precut 1 yard (91.4 cm) of fabric into four *fat quarters*, which they sell individually. Each measures half the width and length of the yard, approximately 18 x 22 inches (45.5 x 56 cm). Quilt shops often bundle complementary colors and prints into fat quarter collections.

Non-Wool Fabrics

Since so many terrific non-wool fabrics exist, why not indulge in a little fiber mixing? As long as the care requirements and the general weight of the fabrics are the same, you can introduce a cotton backing, silk appliqué, or satin binding. Just avoid using stretch fabrics, heavily textured fabrics, bulky fabrics, and open weaves. Here's a short list of some popular fabrics suitable for quilting.

Chintz is a cotton fabric with a glazed surface.

Cotton broadcloth and *calico* are basic quilting fabrics available in a wide range of colors and prints. Choose 100 percent cotton fabrics: they're easier to work with and less prone to puckering at the seams than cotton/polyester blends, although the blends do wash nicely.

Satin, sateen, and *charmeuse* are satin-weave fabrics with a soft, lustrous hand. They're typically made of silk, polyester, acetate, or rayon fibers. These fabrics can be slippery, so lots of pins and special sewing techniques might be necessary. While sewing, use a straight-stitch or even-feed presser foot. Loosen the upper thread tension slightly and hold the fabric taut as it moves through the machine to minimize puckering. You can also stabilize them with foundation paper or tear-away stabilizer.

Silk broadcloth, dupioni, and *shantung* are silk fabrics that work well with wool. They add sheen and elegance to quilted projects.

Thread

Repeat after me: avoid cheap thread—it's inexpensive for a reason. Good-quality thread is strong, smooth, and with uniform thickness, and it doesn't produce a lot of lint. It's certainly worth the investment, and it's not like it costs a lot in the first place. Cotton/polyester threads are best suited to sewing with wool fabrics; you can, however, use cotton thread for decorative stitching. Color, of course, is up to you—whether you want it to match or contrast. If you want subtle stitching, use invisible nylon thread, which comes in clear and smoke shades.

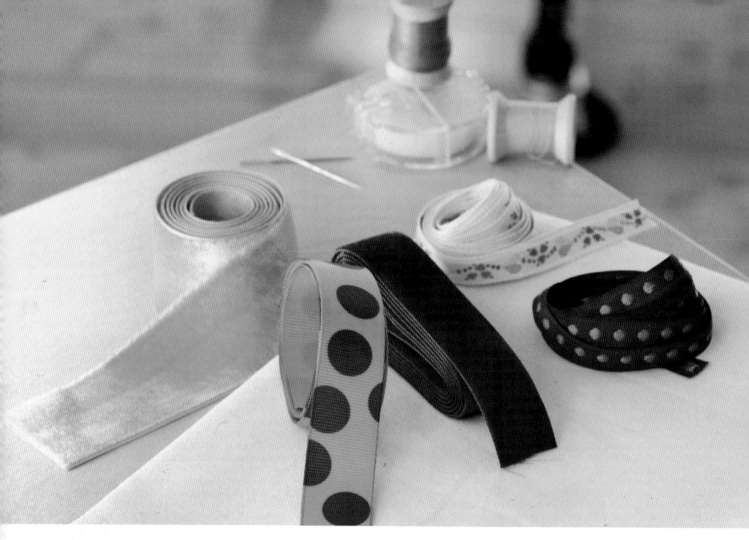

Support Fabrics

Some fabrics, particularly sweater knits, slippery fabrics, and some lighter weight wools, benefit from the addition of a backing fabric that makes the tricky fabric easier to sew and produces a crisper, sturdier finished item.

Interfacing adds invisible, permanent body and stability to your fashion fabric. It can be sewn or fused in place (refer to the packaging instructions for how to apply fusible interfacing). Choose one that is lighter weight than the fashion fabric so it supports but doesn't change the hand of the fabric. The project instructions indicate whether interfacing is necessary.

Stabilizers come in several forms—tear-away, wash-away, iron-away, and cut-away. They're typically used under decorative stitching to support the stitches. Once the fabric is stitched, the stabilizer is removed. You can also use these products to stitch slippery and lightweight fabrics and then remove them once the project is complete.

Embellishments

Don't you just love to give your sewing projects special flair by adding trims and novelties? Take a walk through the ribbon and notions department of your local fabric store—it's too much fun! Don't forget about beads, charms, lace, piping, and any other trims. Sometimes an entire project can be designed around an exotic ribbon or beautiful vintage buttons. Even just the simple selection of a heavier or shiny thread can make a huge difference in the appearance.

Choose your embellishments so they have the same care requirements as the fabrics. You don't want to use dry-clean-only upholstery fringe on a blanket that you'll want to wash frequently, but it could be perfect on a pillow or handbag. Wool roving (wool in fiber form) can be stitched or needle felted to a base cloth for visual interest.

Basic Tool Kit

You won't need a lot of fancy tools. In fact, you probably own everything you need.

Basic Sewing Kit

You'll need these basic items to make all the projects in this book:

- Sewing machine and needles
- Thread
- Straight pins
- Sewing scissors
- Shears or rotary cutter/cutting mat/ruler
- Measuring tape
- Seam ripper
- Hand-sewing needles
- Iron and ironing board
- Pencil
- Fabric marker or tailor's chalk

Sewing Machine

A sewing machine that sews straight and zigzag stitches and has a stitch length adjustment is fundamental. Most standard seaming is 10 to 12 stitches per inch (2.5 cm). Use a longer stitch, 7 to 10 stitches per inch (2.5 cm), when you're sewing multiple layers. If a project requires a different stitch length, it will be noted in the instructions.

It's not necessary for this book, but what a bonus if you can drop the feed dogs (the teeth located below the presser foot) on your machine. These move the fabric through the machine. Free-motion quilting, an exciting technique that's a little like painting with thread, requires that you either drop the feed dogs or cover them.

Sewing machine needles should be replaced frequently, after every six to ten hours of sewing. It's a good idea to have several sizes and types on hand because you never know when a needle might break. (Of course, as long as you don't sew over your pins, you probably won't break a needle!) Needle size 80/12 is a good size to start with; drop down to size 70/10 for fine fabrics and go up to size 90/14 for heavier fabrics.

On Pins and Needles

Straight pins, quilting pins—which are longer than straight pins—and safety pins are essential for holding layers together before you sew.

Universal needles are good for general machine sewing and for piecing quilt shapes. If you're sewing multiple layers by machine, you might want to use a quilting needle, which is very sharp, so it penetrates all those layers easily. Or, if you're machine sewing with heavier, decorative thread, switch to an embroidery needle, which has a large eye.

And, of course, you must have hand-sewing needles. Sharps are perfect for most hand sewing, although it's a good idea to have hand-embroidery needles (with a larger eye) so you can work with embroidery floss or heavy threads.

Presser Feet

Every machine comes with a general-purpose foot that's suitable for most sewing, and a zipper foot that's used to install zippers. Specialty presser feet aren't necessary, but they're helpful. A quarter-inch foot is the perfect stitching guide because the edge of the foot falls exactly ¼ inch (6 mm) away from the edge of the fabric. An *even-feed* or *walking foot* feeds multiple layers through the machine evenly to minimize shifting, puckering, and skipped stitches.

Measuring Tools

Transparent rulers with gridded measurements and angles printed on the surface are one tool that you'll wonder how you ever lived without. You can also use these rulers as a straightedge when you're cutting with a rotary cutter. A good basic ruler is 6 x 24 inches (15 x 61 cm). You should also have a plastic tape measure on hand.

Marking Tools

Fabric marking pencils, fabric chalk, and disappearing ink markers are easy to use and then easy to remove. Test any marking tool near the edge of the fabric to make sure it comes off before you start marking. Keep an old-fashioned lead pencil nearby, too.

Cutting Tools

To cut accurately, you'll need a couple of cutting tools. Shears measure 7 to 8 inches (17.8 to 20.3 cm) long, have bent handles, and are used to cut long lengths of fabric. Sewing scissors are 6 inches (15.2 cm) long with one sharp tip and are a basic and essential sewing tool. Thread snips are 3 to 4 inches (7.6 to 10.2 cm) long with two sharp tips; they're really handy for cutting thread ends.

A rotary cutter is used with a cutting mat (which is often printed with a measuring grid) to cut smooth edges through multiple fabric layers. A small rotary cutter is best for cutting curves; select a larger one for cutting straight edges. Be sure to apply the safety or blade lock when you're not using it.

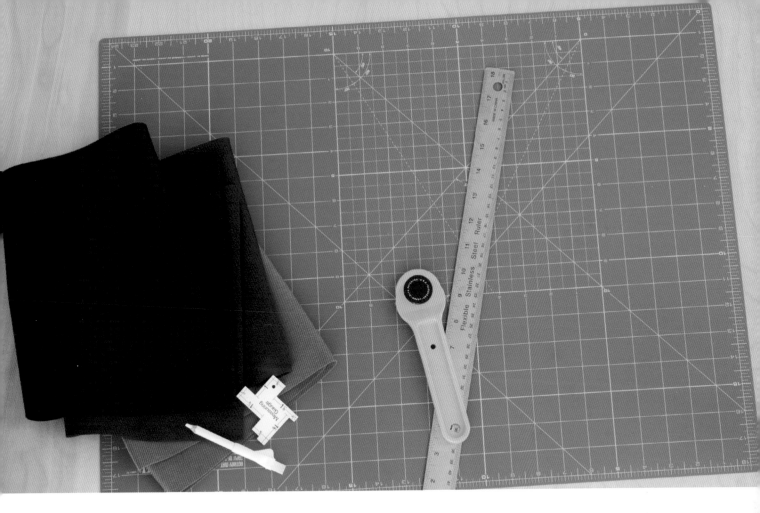

A seam ripper is indispensable. No matter how experienced he or she is at sewing, every sewer has to pull out stitches sometimes. This tool makes it easy and protects the fabric from accidental scissor snips.

Pressing Tools

You'll definitely need a steam iron and an ironing board for every project. A scrap of muslin or cheesecloth, or a clean white handkerchief, makes a suitable press cloth to protect both the fabric and the iron's soleplate. Since you'll be using steam when you press your wool projects, a bottle of distilled water will protect your iron from mineral buildup. If you have one, a *seam roll* makes it easier to press seams open without leaving a visible seam edge on the right side of the fabric.

Large Work Surface

It helps to have a large work surface to arrange quilt designs. You might place a bed sheet on the floor if you need a really large design space. To make sewing a little easier, position your sewing machine on the right side of your worktable, so there's more room to the left to support the fabric as you sew. Finally, for larger quilts, consider hanging a piece of cotton flannel on the wall or on the back of a door; your fabric shapes will adhere to the flannel without pins.

A man's wool suit weighs about 4 pounds (1.8 kg). (No wonder so many guys don't want to dress up.)

Getting Started

Whether you're making an entire quilt or a smaller quilted novelty, the techniques will be similar. Not every technique is used in every project, but the following techniques provide a basic understanding of the quilting craft.

Prep Work

Before cutting, prepare your fabrics, trims, and batting. If you're using cotton backing or other cotton fabrics, machine wash and dry them, and press to remove wrinkles. If you're using silk or satin, dry-clean or hand wash them in cold water with mild detergent. It's also a good idea to hand wash trims in cold water with mild soap to preshrink them and remove excess dyes. If you're using batting, note the manufacturer's recommendations because some batting should be washed and dried before it is used.

Wool, on the other hand, should be hand washed in cold water and mild detergent, or machine washed in the delicate cycle. Press the wool by setting the iron to the wool setting and fill the reservoir with distilled water. Wool requires more steam than heat. Press with an up and down motion (instead of the gliding motion of ironing) to avoid stretching or distorting the fabric shape. The iron can cause surface shine, so use a press cloth between the iron and the fabric. If you inadvertently cause fabric shine from the iron, avoid a press mess by sponging the fabric surface with a clean cloth and white vinegar. Rinse out the vinegar.

Upcycled Fabric

Press the garment, blanket, or whatever you're cutting apart to remove wrinkles that might distort the shape and size of the cut pieces. If you're "harvesting" fabric from a garment, cut away seams, zippers, buttons, and labels with scissors. Rough-cut the largest possible piece of smooth fabric and press it again. Establish a clean, straight edge to measure from by aligning the cut edges with a straight line on a gridded mat or ruler. Mark and cut along the straight line.

Before and after machine washing a sweater in hot water and soap to felt it.

Felting Wool

Think of felting wool as tangling the fibers into a dense mat. This couldn't be simpler. Just toss your 100 percent wool sweater or fabric into the washing machine with a clean pair of jeans and mild laundry detergent. Set the appliance for a hot wash cycle and cold rinse cycle. The hot water, soap, and agitation do the job. The longer the cycles, the more the fibers felt together, so check the wool periodically. Remove it when it has felted enough, or keep it in the washer to felt it even more (you can even run it through the wash multiple times). Then, partially or completely dry the wool in the dryer—it stops felting once you remove it from either the washer or the dryer. If it's still damp, lie it flat on a towel to finish drying. Notice how you've completely changed the hand of the fabric: it's thicker and stiffer.

Piecing

There are many ways to create a quilted design. The most obvious quilting technique is piecing, in which small shaped pieces of fabric are sewn together to form a pattern or unique design. Pieced quilt designs are made by stitching together specific fabric pieces with ¼-inch (6 mm) seams (unless otherwise noted), and a

Generally, an ordinary Australian sheep will yield 5 to 6 pounds (2.3 to 2.7 kg) of wool per shearing. A pound of wool can be spun into up to 20 miles (32.2 km) of yarn!

short stitch length of about 15 stitches per inch (2.5 cm). Instead of backstitching at the beginning and end of a seam, shorten the stitch length for the first and last few stitches. There's no need to trim the seam allowance, unless directed to do so, although you'll need to trim away corners and extending triangle points.

To ease and keep a curved seam smooth, snip— with the tips of your small scissors—into the seam allowance, up to, but not through, the stitching. Snip about every ¼ inch (6 mm) or more if the seam is particularly curved, and less if it isn't.

Make sure the seams match up by inserting a pin through both of them and then removing the pins as you sew. As you piece the fabrics, finger press the seams. (To avoid distortion, you shouldn't press with an iron until the piece has straight grain on all sides.) If you're pressing intersecting seams, minimize bulk by finger pressing them so the seam allowances face opposite directions. If seams don't intersect, press all the seam allowances to one side, usually toward the darker fabric.

Once the design is complete, remove any markings that could be heat set by the iron. As a general rule, press the wrong side first and then the right side, using more steam than pressure. Remember to use an up and down—not a back and forth—motion.

Appliqué

Appliqués are shaped pieces of fabric that you cut from a pattern or template and stitch or fuse onto a foundation fabric or garment. The laptop cozy on page 38, for example, is appliquéd with a felt log.

Fuse and Stitch Appliqué

Fuse a piece of paper-backed adhesive bonding to the wrong side of the appliqué fabric. Mark the desired shape on the paper side of the bonding, using the template provided. Cut out the shape, remove the paper backing, and fuse it to the foundation fabric following the manufacturer's instructions. Machine or hand stitch around the edge of the appliqué with any number of stitches. Machine zigzag is popular because it covers the raw edge, but a blanket stitch looks lovely, too.

Turn and Stitch Appliqué

If the appliqué isn't too curved, press the raw edge under ¼ inch (6 mm). Slipstitch, zigzag, or decorative stitch the folded edge to the foundation fabric.

Line and Stitch Appliqué

It's challenging to fold a smooth edge on curved shapes and circles. Instead, cut the appliqué shape from the desired fabric and from a piece of tulle (that's the netting used for making tutu skirts), but cut both pieces ¼ inch (6 mm) larger all around than the desired appliqué shape. With right sides together, stitch around the entire perimeter of the appliqué. Carefully cut a small slit in the middle of the tulle and trim the seam allowance to about ⅛ inch (3 mm). Turn the appliqué right side out by pulling it through the slit in the tulle. Roll and flatten the seam allowance to make a smooth edge around the appliqué; press (figure 1). Stitch the appliqué in place by hand or machine.

figure 1

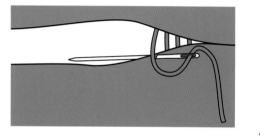

figure 2

figure 3

figure 4

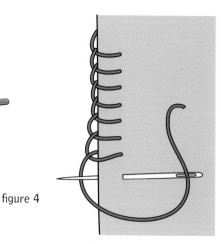

All Torn Up

Tearing fabric instead of cutting it creates a straight, soft, raw edge, as long as you tear across the width of the fabric, from selvage to selvage. Make a little snip, between 1/2 and 1 inch (1.3 and 2.5 cm) into the selvage, grasp the fabric on either side, and pull outward to tear across the width of the fabric at that point.

Machine Stitches

Staystitching is used to prevent fabric from stretching. Simply stitch within the seam allowance, parallel to the fabric edge.

Edgestitch is a visible machine stitch done very close to a seam or fabric fold. It is not meant to be decorative, but it holds the seam allowance in place or keeps a fold from rolling. It also adds crispness to the seam.

Topstitching is visible, and usually decorative stitching. It can be done anywhere on an item, either by machine or by hand. Unlike edgestitching, which is more functional, topstitching is usually done with contrast or heavy thread so that it stands out.

Basting can be done by machine, by adjusting for the longest possible stitch length, or by hand. It's a series of long straight stitches with equally long spaces between the stitches.

Hand Slipstitch

This invisible stitch is used to close openings and to attach appliqués. Press the seam allowances to the wrong side. Insert the needle and thread inside one of the seam allowances so the knot is buried inside. Bring the needle out through the fold, insert the needle into the fold directly across, and let the needle travel along the fold for about 1/4 inch (6 mm). Push the needle out through the fold. Repeat, taking stitches across the opening, through the fabric folds, or between the appliqué and the background fabric until the opening is sewn closed or the appliqué is stitched in place (figure 2).

Decorative Stitches

With so many threads to choose from, you can add beautiful stitching to everything. Anything goes! Cotton embroidery floss is traditional and can be separated into varying thicknesses. Pearl cotton is heavy, perfect for covering large areas. Silk and rayon threads have a beautiful sheen and softness. Wool yarns add a homespun touch. Experiment with different threads and stitches for a whole world of design options.

Running Stitch

This broken line of straight stitches looks even bolder with heavier thread (figure 3).

Blanket Stitch

A perfect edge-finishing stitch, blanket stitch is often used at hems and to attach appliqués (figure 4).

figure 5

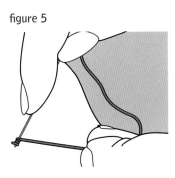

figure 6

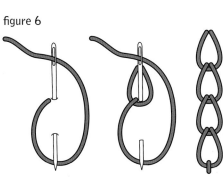

figure 7

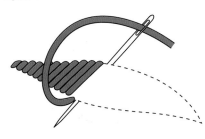

French Knot

This elegant knot is a real show-off. Keep your thread tight as you embroider it (figure 5).

Chain Stitch

The linked loops of this stitch can be used in place of the straight stitch to outline a design, or in place of the satin stitch to fill in a specific area (figure 6).

Satin Stitch

Keep these closely spaced, filling stitches less than 1 inch (2.5 cm) long, or they might snag (figure 7).

Stacking the Layers

If you've created a quilted design but aren't making a quilt, refer to the project instructions for how (or whether) you need to add batting and backing layers.

However, if you're working on a multilayer quilted project, you'll need to assemble the layers before you stitch them together.

1 Once you've completed the design or the front of the project, trim the backing and batting to the same size as the front.

2 Place the three layers together: quilt top, then batting, and finally backing fabric, with the right sides of the quilt top and backing facing out. This is the quilt sandwich.

3 Pin the layers together with safety pins, starting in the center of the quilt. Place the pins about 4 inches (10.2 cm) apart so the layers don't shift. If you prefer, you can hand baste the layers together, again starting from the center and working toward the sides, but pin and smooth the layers first.

Joining the Layers

Once the layers are arranged—do note, some of these projects have only one or two layers—you have to join them (or it) to each other or to another fabric. You can stitch them by hand with quilting thread and a lot of patience, or you can stitch them by machine. Or opt to simply tie the layers together with strategically placed knots.

Quilting

If you're in no hurry and treasure the hand-quilted look, quilt the traditional way, needle in hand. It's totally acceptable to go with machine sewing, though.

Machine Quilting

When machine quilting, position your hands one on each side of the presser foot to guide and ease the fabric layers, and to prevent shifting or the formation of unwanted tucks. Rely on the feed dog and the presser foot to help move the fabric in straight, long lines or gentle curves through the machine. (A walking or even-feed presser foot helps even more.) Typically, machine quilting is done with straight machine stitches, but any decorative stitch can be used. At the beginning and end of each line of stitching, adjust the stitch length to zero to secure the stitching, and then increase it to the desired stitch length for the remainder of the stitching.

If your project is large, keep things manageable by rolling up one side toward the center so the project fits under the arm of the sewing machine. Stitch the central areas, and then partially unroll the project. Stitch the next line or area, and continue in this manner. Once you've stitched the entire side, turn the project 180° and repeat to stitch the other side.

Quilted designs may be all over, or they can punctuate specific areas. They can outline the shapes in a pieced design or have absolutely no relation to them.

If you're quilting a design that's independent from your pieced designs, draw it onto the quilt top with a fabric marker *before* assembling the quilt sandwich. Here are a few tried-and-true styles of quilting.

Stitch-in-the-Ditch

This defines or emphasizes the design. It's the easiest way to stitch a quilt because you simply stitch directly over existing seams. If you're machine quilting, don't look at the needle as you sew. Instead, look about 1 to 2 inches (2.5 to 5.1 cm) in front, so you can keep the needle centered over the seam.

Outline Quilting

This is also known as echo quilting. Straight stitching, done ¼ inch (6 mm) away from the seam of a pieced design, outlines its shape. This is easier to do on small quilted projects because you have to pivot the fabric a lot. Either mark the stitching line directly on the fabric with chalk or a disappearing ink pen, or use the edge of your presser foot—as long as it's ¼ inch (6 mm) from the needle—as a guide. When you come to a corner or an angle, stop ¼ inch (6 mm) away *with the needle down in the fabric.* Raise the presser foot, pivot the fabric, lower the presser foot, and continue stitching.

Channel Quilting

In this quilting style, parallel lines of stitching create a furrowed effect. Draw the first stitching line in the center of the project. You can mark all the subsequent stitching lines the same distance apart, or use a quilting bar attachment that affixes to the presser foot and extends a determined distance away to ensure straight, parallel stitching (without marked guidelines).

figure 8

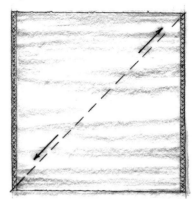

figure 9

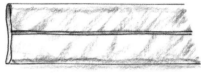

figure 10

figure 11

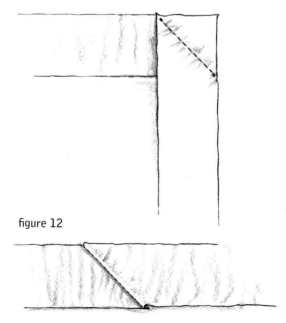

figure 12

Tying

Tying simply consists of a series of knots strategically placed to keep the layers from shifting. The thread should be strong and the knots must be secure. You can machine or hand tie the layers together.

Hand Tying

To tie by hand, you'll need a large-eyed needle and thread, yarn, or even ribbon. Decide which side of the quilt will feature the knots, and mark their locations with a disappearing ink pen. Next, starting in the center of the piece and working outward, insert your needle at the marking, taking it through all the layers, and bring it back out at the entry point. Repeat a second time so the knot will be more secure. Cut the yarn or thread so you have two 2-inch (5.1 cm) lengths and tie them in a square knot.

Machine Tying

This process is similar to hand tying. Start by marking the tie or knot locations. Then, machine stitch eight to ten zigzag stitches very close together at each location (set the stitch length and width to zero). This makes a thread knot with no tie ends. If you prefer visible ties, cut 3- to 6-inch (7.6 to 15.2 cm) lengths of ribbon and attach the center of each ribbon over the marking, again with several zigzag stitches. Tie the ribbon into a bow to cover the stitches.

Binding a Quilted Project

The edges of many quilted projects are clean-finished so they'll look attractive and the stitching won't come apart. Encasing edges with trim or binding is a good, sturdy finish, and there are several ways to do it. It's a good idea to use an even-feed or a walking presser foot (page 18).

Making Binding

You can purchase commercial bias binding or quilt binding, but it's easy to make your own so it matches or complements the project perfectly. For a quilted project with straight edges, the binding doesn't have to be cut on the bias grainline; if it has any curved edges, however, bias binding is better for smooth, pucker-free binding. The bias grainline is diagonal to the selvage and provides the greatest amount of stretch in a woven fabric (see below).

- To make *straight binding*, fold your fabric in half with the selvages together and cut cross-grain strips to the desired width, parallel to the cut edge.
- To cut *bias binding*, mark the bias grainline at a 45° angle to the selvage. Draw cutting lines parallel to the bias marking at the desired width; cut along the markings (figure 8).

How wide should you cut the bias binding?

- For *single fold* (for small projects), cut strips four times the desired width. After cutting it, press the binding strips in half lengthwise with the wrong sides together. Unfold the strip and press both long edges so they meet at the pressed center fold (figure 9).
- For *double fold* (used for quilts and large projects), cut four times the desired width. After cutting the strips, take the same steps as for single-fold binding, and then fold the single-fold binding in the center again and press the center fold (figure 10).

You might need to piece several strips to get the total length necessary for binding a project. Place the end of one strip over the other at a right angle with the right sides together. Stitch diagonally from one corner to the opposite corner of the overlapping squares (figure 11). Cut off the corners, leaving 1/4-inch (6 mm) seam allowances. Open and press the allowances flat (figure 12).

Wool is comparatively stronger than steel. It can stretch up to 70 percent without breaking, then return to its original length.

Here's a tip for topstitching: If you choose to topstitch the binding over the raw edge, make it easy by pressing the bias strip lengthwise, but not in half. Instead, press it so that one side is about ⅛ inch (3 mm) wider than the other (figure 13). Then open the strip and press the cut edges so they meet at the pressed crease (figure 14). When you slide the binding over the raw edge, make sure the narrower side is on top; this way, when you topstitch from the right side, you'll be sure to catch the edge of the binding on the bottom because it's slightly wider.

figure 13

figure 14

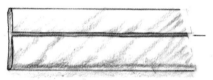

Continuous Binding

This type of binding is done in one continuous seam; the quilts shown on this page feature this type of finish.

1 Baste the layers together, close to the edge, and trim the batting as close as possible to the stitching.

2 Open the seam allowance on one edge of the binding (single or double) and pin it to the quilt with right sides together (you can pin to the front or back of the quilt), starting in the middle of one side. Leave about a 2-inch (5.1 cm) binding tail loose for finishing (figure 15).

figure 15

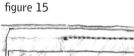

3 Stitch, stopping ¼ inch (6 mm) away from the corner, and backstitch. Cut the threads. Pull the fabric out from under the needle and fold the binding straight up, forming a right angle (figure 16).

figure 16

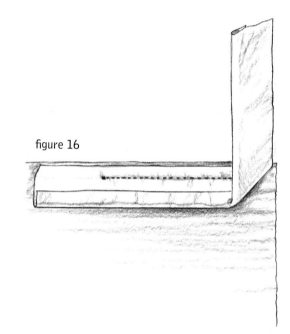

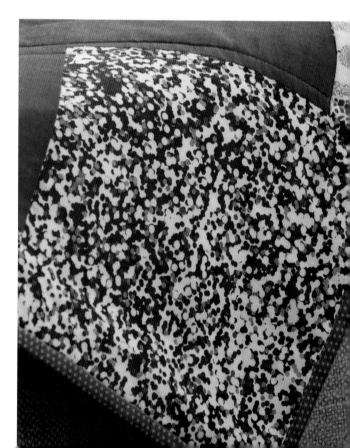

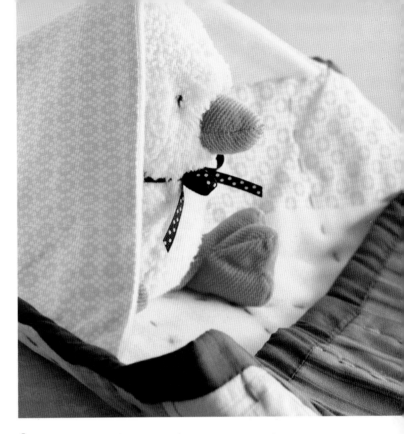

4 Fold the binding again, this time straight over the previous fold, so the edges of the binding and quilt align. Put the pieces back under the needle close to the top edge, and backstitch (figure 17). Stitch to the next corner and repeat the miter process at each corner.

figure 17

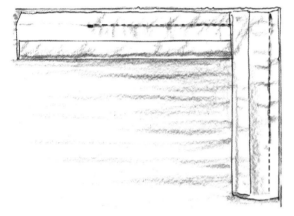

5 Stop stitching about 8 inches (20.3 cm) away from the beginning of the binding strip, and backstitch (figure 18). Pull the project out from the machine. Lay the binding strips over each other and pin mark them together somewhere in the overlap. Open up the bindings and sew them with right sides together at the pin marks. Trim the extra binding away. Refold the binding and finish sewing it to the quilt.

figure 18

An experienced shearer can remove the fleece from a sheep in merely two to three minutes.

6 Fold the binding over the quilt edge. A miter will form on the stitched side, but on the unstitched side, fold the corner diagonally and then fold each side to meet in the center and pin the miter in place. Hand stitch the folded edge to the quilt, taking care to stitch the mitered corner edges together (figure 19).

figure 19

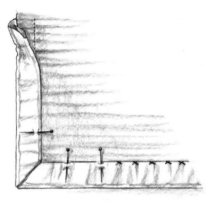

Binding corners isn't hard; it just takes a little time. You might want to consider softening corners if you want to take a shortcut (or just like the appearance of the curves). Just trace around a plate or a bowl with a fabric marking pen to round off the angles. Then you won't have to miter the binding: you can simply ease it around the bend.

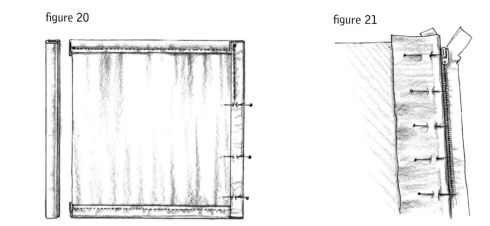

figure 20 figure 21

Topstitched Binding

Topstitched binding is quick. You need four separate binding strips, one for each side of the project, as shown in the project at bottom left.

1 Cut four strips, one for each side and about 1 inch (2.5 cm) longer than each side. Press the strips lengthwise, slightly off center, with the wrong sides together.

2 Place the binding over the edge of the quilt top and quilt bottom. Topstitch close to the folded edge, encasing the raw edge of the quilt and catching the binding in the seam on both the front and the back.

3 Trim the ends even with the project sides. Fold the short ends of the remaining strips ½ inch (1.3 cm) to the wrong side. Repeat step 2 to encase the sides of the project (figure 20).

Making Fabric Ties

Of course you can use cording or ribbon to tie certain projects closed, but sometimes a special fabric that coordinates or contrasts the main fabric is the perfect touch. Use a measuring tape to determine how long you need to make the ties so they wrap the project closed and can still be knotted or tied into a bow.

1 Decide how long and wide you want the ties, and then cut two fabric pieces with the following measurements. The width will be twice the desired finished width plus ½ inch (1.3 cm). The length will be the same as the desired length of the tie plus ½ inch (1.3 cm).

2 Fold each piece in half lengthwise, right sides together, and stitch one long edge using a ¼-inch (6 mm) seam allowance. Turn the pieces right side out.

3 Fold the short ends to the inside and topstitch or hand stitch them closed.

Installing a Lapped Zipper

A lapped zipper has a lip of fabric that covers the zipper so the teeth are completely hidden away from sight. Install a zipper presser foot on your machine.

1 Pin the two pieces with right sides together using a seam allowance 1½ inches (3.8 cm) wide.

2 Stitch the pieces together for ½ to 1 inch (1.3 to 2.5 cm), depending on the length of the zipper and the length of the opening; backstitch. Switch to a basting

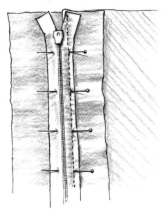

figure 22

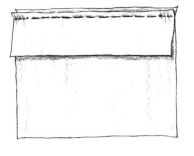

figure 23

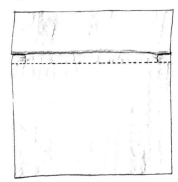

figure 24

stitch and continue across the seam until you are ¹/₂ to 1 inch (1.3 to 2.5 cm) from the edge. Switch the sewing machine back to a regular stitch length and finish stitching the rest of the seam (figure 21).

3 Press the seam open. Fold one of the seam allowances ¹/₄ inch (6 mm) from the seam and press. With the zipper right side up, pin the folded seam allowance onto the zipper tape (figure 22).

4 Install the zipper presser foot on the machine and stitch along the folded piece of fabric ¹/₈ inch (3 mm) from the zipper teeth.

5 Turn the piece over so the wrong side faces up, and fold it along the seam so the seam allowance that isn't yet attached to the zipper extends out. Sew the other side of the zipper to the seam allowance (figure 23).

6 Turn the piece over to the right side and mark a line ³/₄ inch (1.9 cm) to the right of the seam and across the ends of the zipper. Stitch along the marking, through all the layers, including the zipper tape (figure 24).

7 Starting in the center, use the seam ripper to open only the basting stitches. Open the zipper.

Cleaning and Storing Wool

Clean the projects the same way you prewashed the fabrics before you started sewing (page 20). Because you're likely to store wool blankets and clothing during the summer months, make sure they're clean before putting them away. Body oils and even the tiniest food stains attract insects, especially moths, and those moths will eat holes in your wool.

Store wool items in airtight plastic bags or bins with tight-fitting lids. It's better to fold them than to hang them, but you might want to wrap or fold them in white tissue paper to prevent wrinkling. If you're concerned about pests, add cedar chips (instead of strong-smelling mothballs). They're a natural insect repellent. Avoid putting the chips directly on the fabric; instead, hang them in small, loosely woven fabric bags (muslin works well). Store the bags or bins away from direct sunlight and temperature extremes.

In 2007, approximately 35 million pounds of wool were produced in the United States. The biggest producers: Texas and Montana.

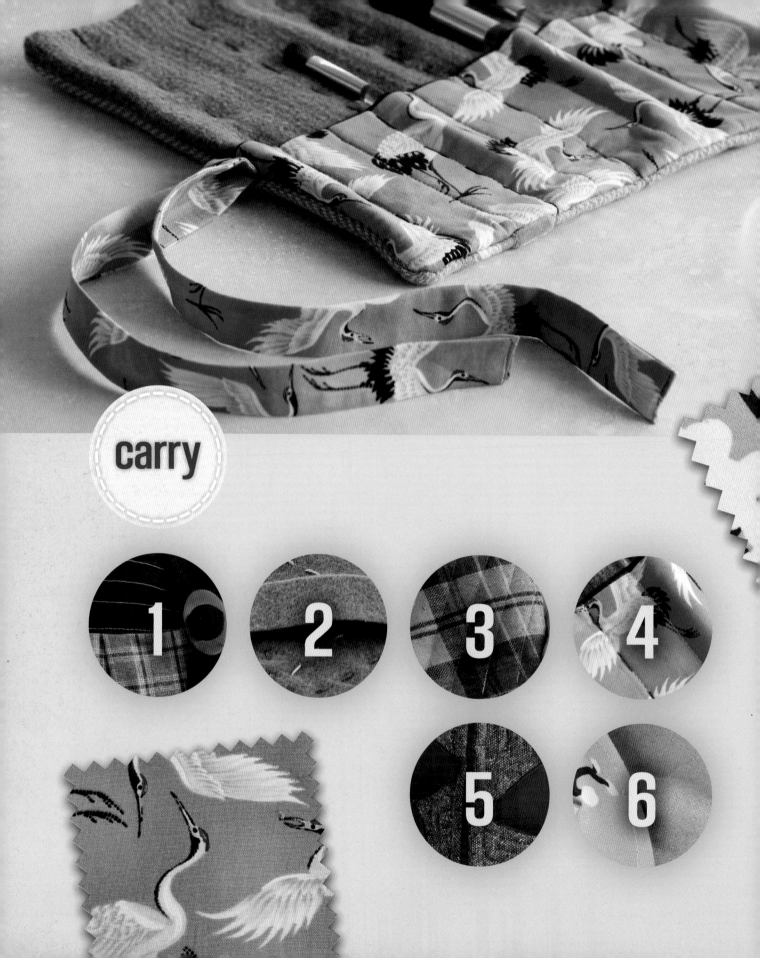

carry

Designer: **Rachel Hayes**

It's all about the details. Spot quilting just at the top of the bag, a lining in a complementary color, the strap end cut on the bias and held by a vintage buckle—these small considerations make for a most intriguing purse.

gather

- ½ yard (45.7 cm) of wool suiting, for bag bottom and handles
- ¼ yard (22.9 cm) of coordinating wool fabric, for bag top and strap
- ½ yard (45.7 cm) of cotton fabric, for lining
- ¼ yard (22.9 cm) of lightweight cotton wadding
- ¼ yard (22.9 cm) of lightweight fusible interfacing
- **Vintage buckle**
- **Basic Sewing Kit (page 17)**
- **Template plastic or thin cardboard**
- **Seam allowance ¼ inch (6 mm) unless otherwise noted**

make

Cut

1 Trace the templates on page 12 onto template plastic or thin cardboard and cut them out.

2 Cut out the following pieces. *Note:* The bag bottom and top templates are cut on the fold of fabric.

From wool suiting: 2 bag bottoms and 4 strips, each 1½ x 18 inches (3.8 x 45.7 cm), for the handles

From coordinating wool fabric: 2 bag tops and 2 straps

From lining: 2 bag bottoms and 2 bag tops

From cotton wadding: 2 bag bottoms

From interfacing: 2 top panels

3 Copy the markings from the templates onto the fabric using chalk or a fabric marking pen.

Exterior

1 Following the manufacturer's instructions, apply fusible interfacing to the wrong side of the top panels.

2 Baste a piece of wadding to the wrong side of each bottom panel. Form the four pleats on each panel by folding at the markings, toward the outside edge. Pin and then baste the pleats in place close to the top edge, being sure to catch both the fabric and the wadding.

3 To make the front of the bag, pin the top edge of the bottom panel (including the wadding) to the lower edge of the top panel (including the interfacing), matching

the centers with right sides together. Stitch, being sure to catch the pleats in the seam. Press the seam allowances toward the top panel and topstitch close to the seam, on the top panel.

4 Pin the two buckle strap pieces right sides together. Stitch along both long edges and the angled edge but leave the short, straight edge open to allow for turning. Turn the strap right side out and press.

5 To make the back of the bag, baste the unfinished ends of the buckle strap to the right side of the bottom panel, as marked on the template. Follow the instructions in step 3, catching the ends of the buckle strap in the seam.

6 Pin the bag front and back right sides together with seams aligned. Stitch the sides and bottom, but leave the top edge unstitched.

7 Pin two of the handle pieces with the right sides together and stitch along both long edges. Turn the handle right side out and press. Repeat to make the other handle.

8 Pin the handles to the top of the bag front and back, at the markings copied from the template. Baste the straps in place, close to the top edge of the bag.

9 To form the bottom corners of the bag, fold the side and bottom seams with the right sides together to form a triangle. Measure and mark a line 2 inches (5.1 cm) from the point and sew across the marking, backstitching at the beginning and end of the seam. Trim close to the stitching and press. Repeat for the other corner (figure 1).

Lining

1 To make the lining for the bag, repeat steps 2 and 3 to make both the front and the back lining pieces, *except* don't use wadding.

2 Pin the lining front and back with the right sides together and the seams aligned. Stitch the sides and bottom, but leave the top edge unstitched and leave a 6-inch (15.2 cm) gap in the stitching on one side. Form the corners by following step 9.

3 Place the bag made from the fashion fabric inside the lining bag so the right sides are together and the handles and buckle strap are positioned well inside to avoid catching them in the seam. Sew around the top edge of the bags.

4 Turn the bag right side out through the opening in the lining. Press the seam and the lining to the inside of the bag. Topstitch close to the edge around the top of the bag. Slipstitch the opening in the lining closed.

Finish

1 Using tailor's chalk, mark three evenly spaced horizontal lines, about ½ inch (1.3 cm) apart, across the top panel. Machine quilt along the lines, through all the layers.

2 Hand stitch the buckle to the center front of the bag, on top of the seam, and feed the buckle strap through.

figure 1

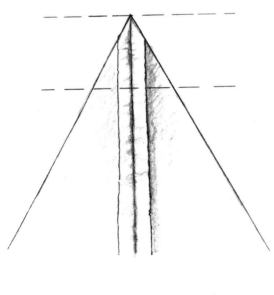

Designer: **Rebeka Lambert**

*In an unusual twist, the motif on the lining fabric guides the design
of the quilting lines that show on the felt exterior of an eyeglass case.*

gather

Wool felt, 9 x 12 inches (22.9 x 30.5 cm)

Printed fabric, 9 x 12 inches (22.9 x 30.5 cm),
   for the lining

2 colors of embroidery floss

Basic Sewing Kit (page 17)

Pinking shears

Embroidery needle

No specific seam allowance

make

1 Use the template on page 118 to cut one front and
one back piece from both the felt and the lining fabric.
Trim all the edges of the lining fabric with the pinking shears. Additionally, cut a piece of felt that's ³⁄₄ x 5
inches (1.9 x 12.7 cm) for the strap.

2 With the wrong sides together, pin the back pieces
together. Do the same with the front pieces.

3 Using the motif printed on the fabric as a guide, use
running stitch (page 22) to hand quilt around the design
with two colors of embroidery floss.

4 Pin the front and back together with the lining sides
together and the bottom edges aligned.

5 Position the felt strap about 1 inch (2.5 cm) from
the top edge of the front piece, indicated with a dotted
line on the template. Insert the short ends between
the layers of the case so the strap will be caught in the
stitching. Make sure the strip isn't so tight that the back
flap can't fit under it to hold the case closed (figure 1).
Start at one bottom corner and edgestitch around the
perimeter of the case, through all the layers, catching
the strap in the seam.

figure 1

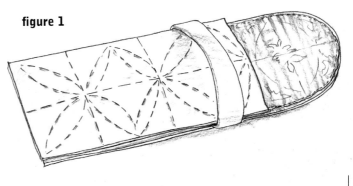

Protect your laptop in a lumberjack-plaid case decorated with a
cute timber-inspired appliqué. Slide it out, and you're ready to log on.

gather

1 yard (90 cm) of wool fabric
1 yard (90 cm) of muslin
1 yard (90 cm) of batting
2 inches (5.1 cm) of black elastic,
    $\frac{1}{4}$ inch (6mm) wide
White thread
Small piece of brown felt, for the appliqué
1 button with 2-inch (5.1 cm) diameter
Basic Sewing Kit (page 17)
Seam allowance $\frac{1}{2}$ inch (1.3 cm)
    unless otherwise noted

make

1 Cut two rectangles of wool, two of muslin, and two of batting, all 2 to 3 inches (5.1 to 7.6 cm) wider and longer than the size of your laptop. Mark the top and bottom edges of the wool fabrics with a disappearing ink fabric marker.

2 To make the back, hand baste the batting to the wrong side of the muslin along the top edge. Pin the wool fabric and muslin with right sides together along the top edge.

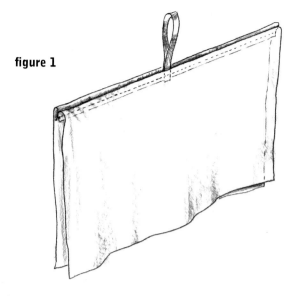

figure 1

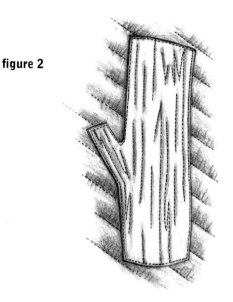

figure 2

3 Measure and mark the center of the top edge. Fold the black elastic into a loop and sandwich it between the wool and the muslin at the marking so the loop extends toward the center of the cover. Sew across the top edge, through all the layers, with a zigzag stitch. Turn the fabrics right side out and press the seam so it rests slightly toward what will be the inside of the cover, as shown in figure 1.

4 To make the front, repeat steps 2 and 3 with the remaining pieces, omitting the elastic.

Quilt and Embellish

1 Hand baste the layers together along the sides and bottom of both the front and the back pieces.

2 With the wool side up, mark diagonal lines for quilting about ¾ inch (1.9 cm) apart, with a disappearing ink fabric marker, on both pieces. Straight stitch over the markings with white (or contrast) thread to quilt the layers.

3 Copy the appliqué template on page 115 and use it to cut the appliqué out of brown felt. Pin the appliqué in the center of the front cover piece and edgestitch it in place with a straight stitch. Using white thread, add straight and zigzag lines of stitching to create the textured effect of knots and wood grain (figure 2).

Assemble

1 With right sides together, pin the front and back around the sides and bottom. Check that your laptop fits inside. If the cover is too big, trim the pieces to fit.

2 Use a zigzag stitch to sew around the bottom and sides, leaving the top open. Trim away any excess fabric and threads.

3 Turn the cover right side out. Double-check the fit of the laptop inside. Hand sew the button onto the front of the cover opposite the elastic loop.

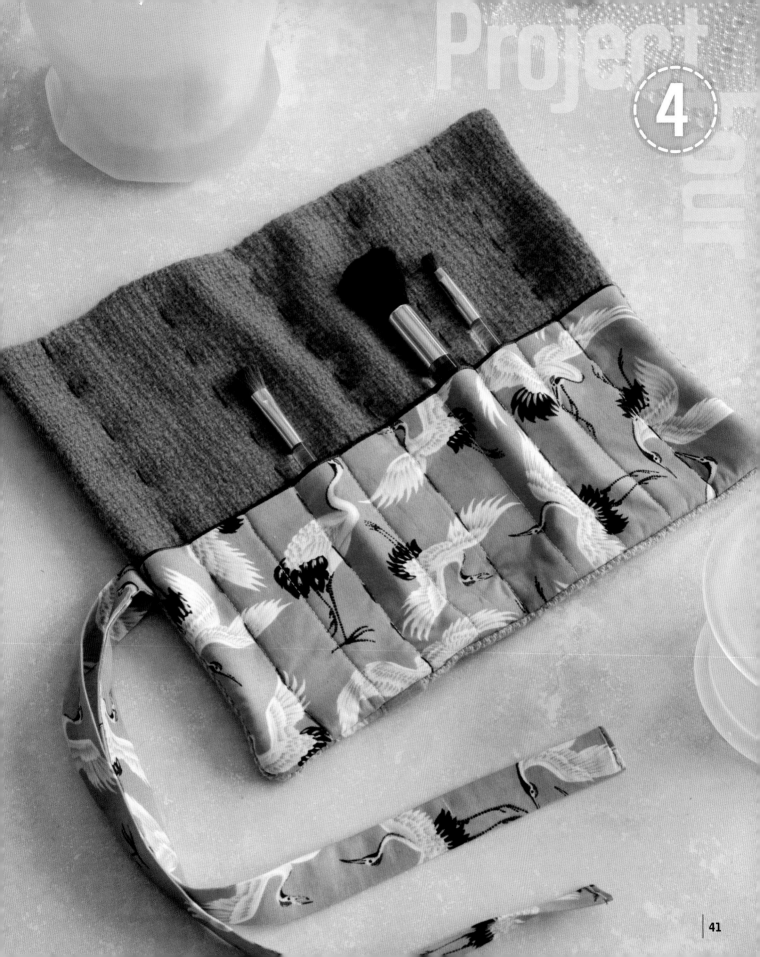

Project Four

Combine an unexpected print with a wool in an unusual colorway—how often do you see blue and white herringbone?—to make a brush holder. Add pretty velvet ribbon and some spot quilting, and you're on a roll.

gather

1 piece of herringbone suiting, 12 x 11 inches
(30.5 x 27.9 cm)

1 piece of wool suiting, 12 x 11 inches
(30.5 x 27.9 cm)

Cotton fabric, 12 x 11 inches (30.5 x 27.9 cm)

Fusible interfacing, 12 x 5½ inches
(30.5 x 14 cm)

12 inches (30.5 cm) of satin piping

12 inches (30.5 cm) of silk velvet ribbon,
1 inch (2.5 cm) wide

Embroidery floss in complementary color

Basic Sewing Kit (page 17)

Zipper presser foot

Embroidery needle

Seam allowance ½ inch (1.3 cm)
unless otherwise noted

make

Cut

1 Select one of the wool rectangles to be the exterior, and one for the interior. Cut two pieces of cotton and one piece of interfacing for the pocket, each 12 x 5½ inches (30.5 x 14 cm).

2 Cut three more pieces from the cotton fabric, two of them 11 x 2¼ inches (27.9 x 5.7 cm) for the front band, and one strip 30 x 2 inches (76.2 x 5.1 cm) to use for the ties.

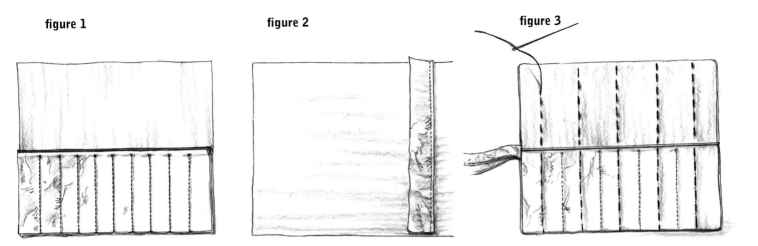

figure 1   figure 2   figure 3

Pocket

1 Following the manufacturer's instructions, fuse the interfacing to the wrong side of one piece of the cotton fabric cut to make the pocket.

2 Pin the two pieces of cotton with the right sides together, sandwiching the piping between the pieces on one long edge, making sure the raw edges of the fabric and piping are aligned. Attach the zipper presser foot, and stitch through all the thicknesses, 1/4 inch (6 mm) from the edge. Turn the pocket right side out and press.

3 Starting 1 1/2 inches (3.8 cm) from the left edge, use tailor's chalk to draw parallel lines approximately 1 1/8 inches (2.8 cm) apart across the fabric to mark the placement of the stitch lines that will form the brush pockets. The rightmost line should be 1 1/2 inches (3.8 cm) from the right side.

4 Pin the pocket fabric to the right side of the suiting selected to be the interior, with the bottom edges aligned. Sew on the marked lines, through all the fabrics, being careful to stop the stitching just before the piping. Backstitch at the piping edge to reinforce the seam (figure 1).

Exterior

1 Pin the two cotton front band pieces right sides together and stitch one of the long edges. Turn right side out and press.

2 Pin the front band vertically (it should run in the same direction as the inside pocket) on the right side of the remaining wool piece, 1/2 inches (3.8 cm) from the right side, with the band seam on the right and the unstitched side on the left. Topstitch the band onto the wool 1/8 inch (3 mm) from the seam (figure 2).

3 Pin the ribbon onto the outside wool piece so that it covers the unfinished edges of the band. Sew along both long edges of the ribbon, through all the layers.

Assemble and Quilt

1 Make one tie end as described on page 28.

2 Pin the wool pieces with the right sides together. Fold the tie in half and sandwich it between the two wool pieces so that the fold of the ties aligns with the raw edges. Position it near the top edge of the inside pocket and on the side closest to the front band and ribbon.

3 Sew around all the edges, being certain to catch the fold of the tie in the seam, leaving a 3-inch (7.6 cm) opening along the bottom edge to allow for turning. Turn the roll-up right side out and press, tucking in the raw edges of the opening. Slipstitch (page 22) the opening closed.

4 Using tailor's chalk and a ruler, draw vertical quilting lines over and extending up from every other pocket stitching line. With six strands of embroidery floss in a needle, hand quilt along the markings (figure 3).

Designer: **Joan K. Morris**

Who says a container has to be rigid? The panels of this soft box feature flower shapes cut from luxe silk; they're emphasized with outline quilting.

gather

½ yard (45.7 cm) of brown tweed
½ yard (45.7 cm) of pink mohair
⅛ yard (11.4 cm) of jacquard-embellished
  wool knit
Scrap of orange silk dupioni
1 yard (90 cm) of felt interfacing
Invisible thread
1 yard (90 cm) of upholstery batting
Kit for making 4 covered buttons, ¾ inch
  (1.9 cm) in diameter
Basic Sewing Kit (page 17)
Spray basting adhesive
Seam allowance ⅝ inch (1.6 cm)
  unless otherwise noted

make

1 Cut five 9-inch (22.9 cm) squares each from the tweed, the mohair, and the felt interfacing. Cut five 8-inch (20.3 cm) squares from the upholstery batting.

2 Using the templates on page 118, cut four flower shapes from the mohair and four circles from the wool knit.

3 Following the manufacturer's instructions, use the spray adhesive to attach a flower in the center of each of four tweed squares. With invisible thread in the needle on your sewing machine and colored thread in the bobbin, zigzag around the edge of the flowers to attach them to the tweed. Position a circle of wool knit in the center of each flower with spray adhesive and zigzag to hold them in place.

4 To make the sides and bottom of the box, create five sandwiches, starting with the felt interfacing on the bottom. Place a piece of batting over each piece of interfacing and then a tweed square (one square doesn't have a flower; it will serve as the bottom of the box) over the batting. Pin the layers together, and then machine baste ½ inch (1.3 cm) from the edges of all five sandwiches.

5 Pin the mohair squares to the sandwiches with the right sides of the tweed and mohair together. Stitch ⅝ inch (1.6 cm) from the edge around all sides, leaving a 5-inch (12.7 cm) opening for turning. Clip the corners and turn the pieces right side out. Press the seams flat, folding the edges of the opening to the inside. Topstitch around the perimeter of each piece, ½ inch (1.3 cm) from the edge, being sure to stitch the opening closed.

figure 1

figure 2

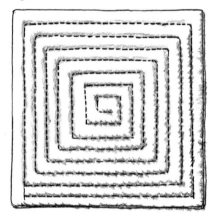

figure 3

6 To quilt the four sides, zigzag again around the edge of each flower, as well as the flower center, with invisible thread in the needle and colored thread in the bobbin. Straight stitch concentrically out from the flower edge, in ¼-inch (6 mm) increments, until the entire tweed background is quilted (figure 1).

7 On the remaining sandwich (the bottom of the box), straight stitch concentrically around the square in ¼-inch (6 mm) increments, working from the perimeter to the center (figure 2).

8 Align the four sides with the bottom, so the edges abut. Using the widest possible zigzag stitch, sew the sides to the bottom (figure 3).

9 Fold up the sides of the box so they meet and hand stitch the inside edges together.

10 Following the manufacturer's instructions, cover the buttons in dupioni silk. Stitch them to the centers of the flowers, hiding the knots under the buttons so they don't show inside the box.

Designer: **Sarah Lalone**

*Subtle diamonds quilt the top of a restrained clutch in pale rose.
But open the purse, and oh!—admire the fresh, cheery print
used for the lining.*

gather

½ yard (45.7 cm) of wool, for the exterior
½ yard (45.7 cm) of heavy cotton,
    for the lining
½ yard (45.7 cm) of lightweight fusible
    interfacing
Magnetic snap set
Basic Sewing Kit (page 17)
Seam allowance ½ inch (1.3 cm)
    unless otherwise noted

make

1 Enlarge the templates on page 115. Cut the fabric, lining, and interfacing as follows:

Wool: Cut 2 pieces of A and 4 pieces of B

Lining: Cut 2 pieces 10½ x 10 inches (26.7 x 25.4 cm)

Interfacing: Cut 4 pieces 11½ x 5½ inches (29.2 x 14 cm)

2 Sew two B pieces, right sides together, along the side edge. Press the seam open and topstitch ⅛ inch (3 mm) on either side of the seam. Repeat with the remaining B pieces.

3 Position the interfacing on the wrong side of all the wool pieces, including the seamed pieces, and trim away any excess. Fuse, following the manufacturer's directions.

4 Sew the bottom of piece A to the top of the seamed B pieces, with right sides together, backstitching at each end. Press the seam allowances toward piece A. Topstitch ⅛ inch (3 mm) from the seam on piece A.

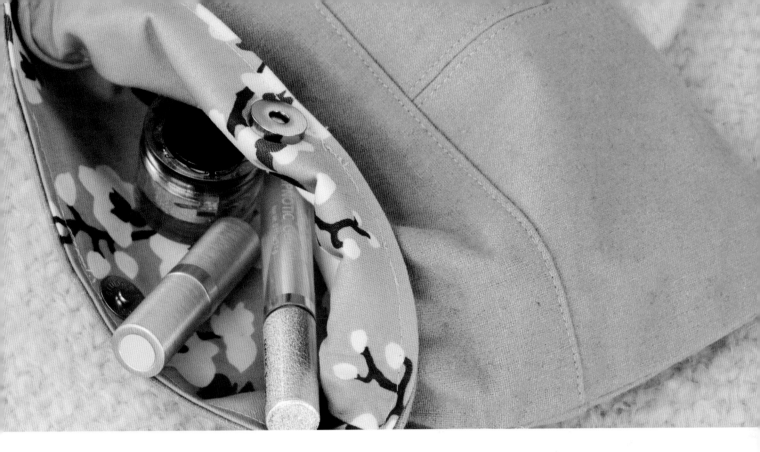

5 Use a ruler and a disappearing fabric marker to draw two diagonal lines on one A piece. To establish the lines, measure and mark along the bottom edge 2 inches (5.1 cm) from the corners, and along the top edge 5 inches (12.7 cm) from the corners. Connect the markings (figure 1).

6 To make a diamond pattern across piece A, measure and mark diagonal lines ³⁄₄ inch (1.9 cm) apart in both directions, using the lines drawn in step 5 as guides. Quilt along the lines, setting the machine to a longer stitch for visual appeal.

7 Pin the lining pieces with the right sides together and sew along three sides, leaving the top open. Press the seams open. Press the top edges 1¹⁄₄ inches (3.2 cm) to the wrong side.

8 Pin the wool pieces with the right sides together and sew along three sides, leaving the top open. Press the top edges ¹⁄₂ inch (1.3 cm) to the wrong side.

9 Insert the lining inside the wool shell with wrong sides together and seams aligned. Center and attach the magnetic snaps to the lining only, about ³⁄₄ inch (1.9 cm) from the top, following the manufacturer's instructions.

10 Topstitch the lining and wool pieces together ³⁄₈ inch (1 cm) from the top edge. This is a flop clutch; fold the quilted top over about 3 inches (7.6 cm) and press it to create a crease.

figure 1

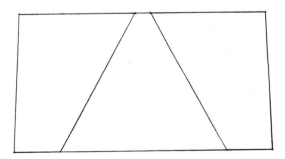

Carry a jumbo-sized bag stitched up in a harlequin pattern and you'll feel larger than life when it comes to fashion.

gather

1 yard (90 cm) of thick orange wool felt
(or 1 French whiskey blanket)
1 yard (90 cm) of navy blue wool felt
1 yard (90 cm) of brown wool felt
56 inches (1.4 m) of cotton cording,
2 inches (5.1 cm) in diameter
6 skeins of navy blue embroidery floss
2 zippers, 14 inches (35.6 cm) long
1 black bar slide (buckle), 1½ inches
(3.8 cm) wide
2 silver key rings, 1 inch (2.5 cm) in diameter
Basic Sewing Kit (page 17)
Zipper presser foot
Embroidery needle
Seam allowance ¼ inch (6 mm)
unless otherwise noted

make

Cut

1 Enlarge the template on page 120.

2 Cut the following pieces.

From the orange felt (or whiskey blanket):
36 squares, 5 x 5 inches (12.7 x 12.7 cm)
1 side/bottom piece, 7 x 52 inches (17.8 cm x 1.3 m)
2 side/top pieces, using the template as the cutting guide

From the blue felt:
24 squares, 5 x 5 inches (12.7 x 12.7 cm)
2 belt pieces, 3 x 38 inches (7.6 x 96.5 cm)
2 handle pieces, using the template as the cutting guide

From the brown felt:
2 front/back pieces, using the template as the cutting guide

Checkerboard

1 Following the schematic (figure 1), machine stitch alternating orange and blue squares, right sides together, to create six strips. Press the seams open. Lay the strips out as shown in the schematic and add one orange square (the one shown at far right in the schematic).

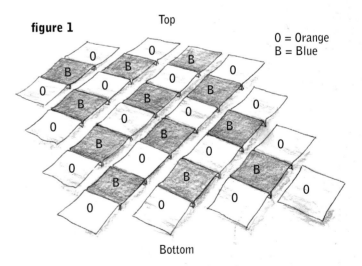

figure 1

Top

Bottom

0 = Orange
B = Blue

2 Stitch the rows with the right sides together, again following the schematic to achieve the checkerboard pattern. Refer to page 21 for how to press and stitch intersecting seams.

3 Repeat steps 1 and 2 with the remaining squares to recreate the exact same thing shown in the schematic a second time.

figure 2

figure 3

figure 4

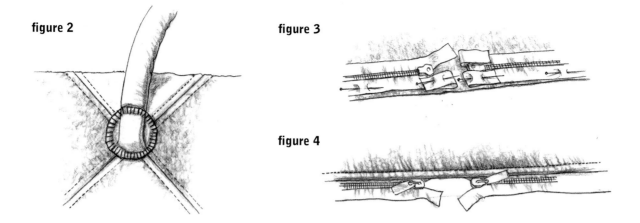

4 Center a brown felt front/back piece on the wrong side of each checkerboard piece. Pin the pieces together, and using the brown felt as a template, cut the checkerboard pieces to the same shape as the brown felt. (Some squares may get cut off.) Baste the two pieces together, 1/2 inch (1.3 cm) from the edge, to make two brown/checkerboard pairs.

Quilt

1 Stitch-in-the-ditch (page 24) over each seam, on both checkerboard pieces. Take care that the brown wool doesn't bunch up.

2 Outline quilt (page 24) inside each square, 1/2 inch (1.3 cm) in from the seams. Set the front and back pieces aside.

Assemble

1 Cut two pieces of cording, each 28 inches (71.1 cm) long. Position a length of cording in the center of one of the blue straps and wrap the strap around the cording; the felt will extend 2 inches (5.1 cm) beyond the cording on both ends. Attach the zipper presser foot to your machine and stitch through the blue felt layers as close as possible to the cording. Fold the extension, or lip, of blue felt down and blanket stitch it in place with embroidery floss.

2 Pin the ends of the handles at the locations marked on the front/back template. Machine stitch around and as close to the edge of the handles as possible. Use embroidery floss to blanket stitch over the machine stitching (figure 2).

3 Pin the bottom/side piece to one of the quilted front and back pieces with the right sides together, starting and stopping at the marks on the pattern. Machine stitch with a 1/2-inch (1.3 cm) seam allowance, leaving 1/2 inch (1.3 cm) of the bottom/side piece unstitched at each end. Ease your stitching around the bottom corners. Repeat to sew the remaining quilted piece to the other side of the bottom/side piece.

4 Pin the zippers facedown, to the right side of the long, marked edge of one of the side/top pieces, so that the pull tabs of each zipper meet in the center of the piece, as shown in figure 3. Pin the extending zipper tape back on itself. The edge of the zipper tape should line up with the edge of the fabric.

5 Using the zipper foot, stitch close to the teeth along the edge of the zipper closest to the cut edge of the fabric. Fold the zipper to the wrong side so the fabric makes a fold. Press that fold and topstitch, close to the fold through all the layers, 1/4 inch (6 mm) from the pressed edge (figure 4).

6 Pin the other half of the zipper tape to the remaining side/top piece as in step 4. Repeat step 5 to attach the remaining side/top piece to the other side of the zipper.

7 Pin the side/top pieces, with the zippers attached, to the top of the bag, with the right sides together, and the zipper pull tabs at the center of the top of the bag. The short ends of the side/top pieces should meet the short ends of the side/bottom pieces, but the wool may have stretched during stitching. If it did, just trim away any excess fabric (and zipper).

figure 5

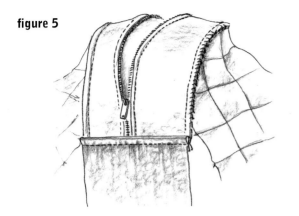
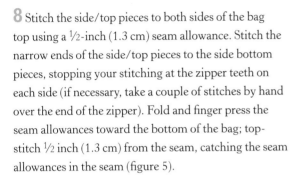

figure 6

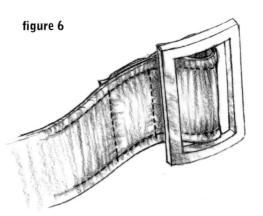

8 Stitch the side/top pieces to both sides of the bag top using a ½-inch (1.3 cm) seam allowance. Stitch the narrow ends of the side/top pieces to the side bottom pieces, stopping your stitching at the zipper teeth on each side (if necessary, take a couple of stitches by hand over the end of the zipper). Fold and finger press the seam allowances toward the bottom of the bag; topstitch ½ inch (1.3 cm) from the seam, catching the seam allowances in the seam (figure 5).

9 Trim the seam allowances as narrow as possible, being careful not to cut into the stitching. Turn the bag right side out. Using embroidery floss, blanket stitch all the way around the checkerboard front and back.

10 Stitch the narrow ends of the belt pieces with right sides together to create one strip about 76 inches (1.9 m) long. Press the strip in half lengthwise and stitch along both long edges. Cut this strip into one piece 52 inches (1.3 m) long for the belt; four pieces 3 inches (7.6 cm) long for the belt loops; and two pieces 4 inches (10.2 cm) long for the key ring pulls.

11 To make the belt loops, press the narrow ends ½ inch (1.3 cm) to the wrong side. Pin and stitch the loops, close to the folded edges, on both the front and the back of the bag, as marked on the template.

12 To make the belt, insert one end around the center of the bar slide buckle and overlap it about 2 inches (5.1 cm). Topstitch a decorative rectangle onto the overlapping sections of the belt to hold the belt and buckle together (figure 6). Trim the other end of the belt to a point and topstitch the newly shaped edges. Run the belt through the belt loops.

13 Fold the key ring pulls in half lengthwise with wrong sides together and stitch along both long edges. Fold a pull over each silver key ring and stitch the layers together to hold them on the key king. Attach the silver key rings to the openings in the zipper pull tabs.

Designer: **Jessie Senese**

Fine chocolate makes the perfect present, but rather than cover a bar in gift wrap, let it stand out by sliding it into a quilted package stitched from an old felted sweater. Add a few vintage buttons to enhance one corner.

gather

1 wool sweater
¼ yard (22.9 cm) of lining or backing fabric
Chocolate bar(s)
Embroidery floss or fine yarn
3 vintage buttons per cozy
Basic Sewing Kit (page 17)
Scrap paper
Wax paper (optional)
Embroidery needle
Seam allowance ¼ inch (6 mm)
   unless otherwise noted

make

1 Felt the sweater (page 20).

2 Measure your chocolate bar. On some scrap paper, draw a pattern that measures the same width as the bar, and double its height plus 1 inch (2.5 cm) for seam allowances and bulk. Use the pattern to cut the sweater, being sure to avoid any ribbing or seams. Also cut a lining/backing fabric. (Or save time by eliminating the lining. The cozies work and look just as good made from felted wool simply decorated with machine-quilted designs. Because the fabric is thick, you don't even need batting to achieve a quilted effect.)

3 Pin the lining and sweater fabrics with right sides together. Stitch all the way around the edges, leaving a 2-inch (5.1 cm) break in the stitching. Turn the cozy right side out and fold the seam allowances of the opening to the inside. Edgestitch (page 22) the opening closed.

4 Quilt the cozy by machine stitching diagonal lines, a grid, or circles, *or* by following an existing pattern on the sweater fabric. You can even create quilting templates by drawing designs on wax paper. Cut them out and iron them, shiny side down, onto the right side of the felt. Machine stitch around the templates, being sure to avoid the wax paper, then peel them off.

5 Press the wool with a very hot iron. The quilt stitching might have distorted the shape, in which case you need to square it up by gently pulling the opposing corners to stretch the fabric. Edgestitch (page 22) around the perimeter of the fabric and press again.

6 Use embroidery floss to sew the buttons in a cluster on the right side of the cozy, near one of the corners and at least ½ inch (1.3 cm) from the edges.

7 Fold the cozy with wrong or lining sides together and stitch it closed along the long edge with embroidery floss or yarn, ½ inch (1.3 cm) from the edge. You can use any stitch to sew it closed; running stitch (page 22) and blanket stitch (page 22) were used here.

8 Remove the outer wrapper from the chocolate bar to expose the foil wrapper. Slide the bar into the cozy. (If you're concerned the recipient might have food allergies, fold up the outer wrapper and slide it into the cozy with the chocolate so the ingredient label can be checked.)

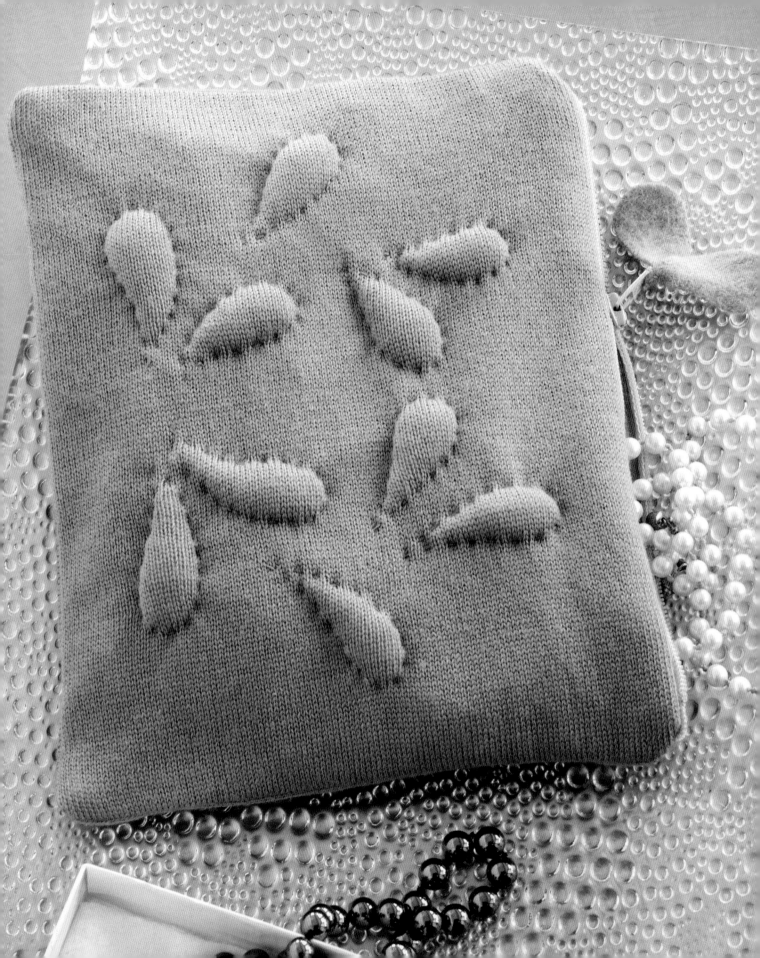

Trapunto is an old, semi-forgotten technique that looks so cool it's being revived by modern stitchers. It involves nothing more than sandwiching a couple of fabrics and quilting an outline, making a small slit in the backing, and firmly stuffing the design to raise it. So little effort for such a pretty pouch.

gather

- 1 fine knit lambswool sweater
- ¼ yard (22.9 cm) of plain cotton fabric, for the backing
- ¼ yard (22.9 cm) of fine cotton lawn, for the lining
- Scrap of felt, for the zipper pull
- Embroidery floss
- Non-washable polyester wadding or wool roving
- 8-inch (20.3 cm) zipper
- Basic Sewing Kit (page 17)
- Transfer paper and marking wheel
- Tapestry needle or tweezers
- Zipper presser foot
- Seam allowance ½ inch (1.3 cm) unless otherwise noted

make

1 Wash and press the lambswool sweater and backing and lining fabrics. Cut two rectangles from the sweater and two from each fabric, each 10 x 8 inches (25.4 x 20.3 cm).

2 Use the transfer paper and marking wheel to transfer the design template on page 116 onto the right side of one piece of backing fabric. Baste the backing pieces to the lambswool pieces, wrong sides together. Set one pair without the marked design aside.

3 Hand baste the outline of the design through both fabric layers. Use a running stitch and one strand of embroidery floss to outline the design. (Start the stitching by fastening the floss in the backing fabric just outside the stitching line.) Remove the basting stitches and press the fabric gently. Separate the fabric layers by pinching the fabrics between your finger and thumb. Cut a small slit in the backing fabric *only*, doing so at the center of each stitched design.

4 Stuff bits of the polyester wadding (or wool roving) into the outlined shapes; use small pieces and start at the exterior edges of the outlined shapes, then work toward the middle. Use a blunt tapestry needle or tweezers to help move the stuffing and fill in the shapes. Slipstitch (page 22) the slits closed with a needle and sewing thread.

5 Attach the zipper to the top of the bag front piece by pinning the top to the finished edge of the zipper tape with the right sides together; hand baste. Using a zipper foot, machine stitch close to the zipper teeth. Fold the top of the bag over the stitching to the right side and press. Repeat to sew the back of the bag to the other side of the zipper.

6 Open the zipper halfway. Pin the bag panels with right sides together and stitch the sides and bottom, catching the zipper tape in the stitching. Backstitch at the beginning and end of the seam.

7 Sew the lining panels with right sides together along the sides and bottom edges. Press the seams flat and the top edges of the lining ½ inch (1.3 cm) to the wrong side.

8 Turn the purse right out. Place the lining inside the purse so the wrong sides are together and slipstitch (page 22) the folded edge of the lining to the zipper tape.

9 Using the template on page 116, cut two zipper tags from the felt. Stitch them to the tip of the zipper pull.

wear

10

11

*Some scarves, you can't help but throw on with a flourish. Back a
patchwork of over-dyed wool with vintage kimono fabric, and
embellish it with hand-stitched quilting in a range of thread colors.*

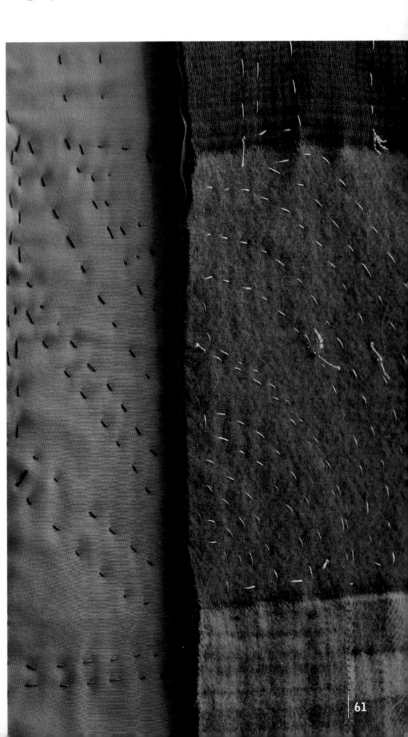

gather

Over-dyed wool in 8 to 10 colors
½ yard (45.7 cm) of silk charmeuse,
     for the backing
½ yard (45.7 cm) of lightweight silk fabric,
     to serve as batting
Rayon threads in contrasting colors
Silk quilting threads in contrasting colors
Basic Sewing Kit (page 17)

Finished Measurements

7 x 65 inches (17.8 x 170 cm)
No specific seam allowance

make

Cut

1 Cut your wool fabric as shown in the schematic
(figure 1, next page). This cutting list is specific to
the scarf pictured here; feel free to vary the length
and width of your wool pieces as desired, to better
use your fabric.

2 Cut two pieces of silk backing, each 8 x 33 inches
(20.3 x 83.8 cm). Repeat with the silk batting fabric.

A, selvedge, ¾ x 7 inches (1.9 x 17.8 cm)

B, 4½ x 7 inches (11.4 x 17.8 cm)

C, 6½ x 7 inches (16.5 x 17.8 cm)

D, 7½ x 4 inches (19 x 10.2 cm)

E, 7½ x 3 inches (19 x 7.6 cm)

F, 6½ x 7 inches (17 x 17.8 cm)

G, 4½ x 7 inches (11.4 x 17.8 cm)

H, 4½ x 7 inches (11.4 x 17.8 cm)

I, ½ x 7 inches (1.3 x 17.8 cm)

J, 6½ x 7 inches (16.5 x 17.8 cm)

K, 4½ x 7 inches (11.4 x 17.8 cm)

L, 7 x 7 inches (17.8 x 17.8 cm)

M, 4 x 7 inches (10.2 x 17.8 cm)

N, 7 x 3½ inches (17.8 x 8.9 cm)

0, 7 x 3½ inches (17.8 x 8.9 cm)

P, selvedge, ¾ x 7 inches (1.9 x 17.8 cm)

figure 1

```
A
B
C
E   D
F
G
H
I
J
K
L
M
O   N
P
```

Sew

1 With right sides together and with a ½-inch (1.3 cm) seam allowance, sew the short ends of the silk backing pieces to make one long piece. Repeat with the silk batting pieces.

2 Arrange and lay out the wool pieces as shown in the schematic, or as desired. Position piece B on the left end of the batting so the edges align. Position piece C next to piece B so the edges abut; *don't* overlap the pieces. Stitch the edges together, through the batting, with a wide zigzag stitch and rayon thread.

3 Zigzag the long edges of pieces D and E together and the long edges of pieces J and K together before attaching them to the batting.

4 Zigzag the remaining squares to the batting, following the schematic. Zigzag the selvedge pieces (a narrow strip of woolen fabric will also work), A and P, to each end of the scarf so they extend beyond the batting.

5 Press the raw edges of the silk backing ¼ inch (6 mm) to the wrong side on all sides. Pin the wrong side of the backing to the scarf, so the batting is between them; use lots of pins to hold the layers together. Use silk thread to quilt the patchwork squares, using running stitch in a variety of patterns, as desired. Then use a running stitch to attach the folded edges of the backing to the perimeter of the scarf, sewing through all the layers.

tip

Over-dyed woolens are available from many Internet sources. You can also over-dye your own thrift-store finds or light-colored woolen fabrics.

Project 11 Eleven

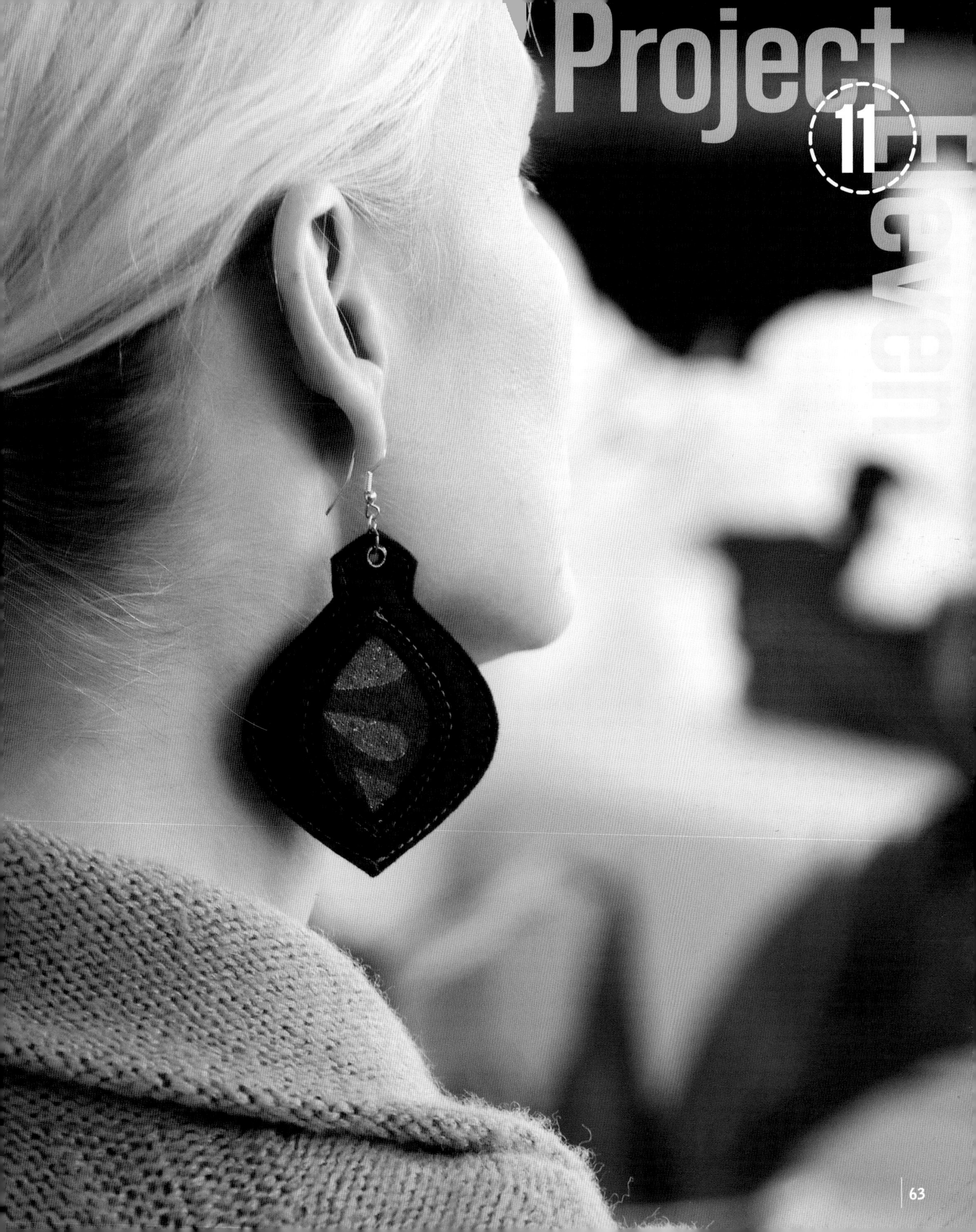

Designer: **Casey Dwyer**

11

To add extra visual interest, stamp the inner area
of a pair of felt earrings with a teardrop pattern.
Part retro and part mod, the lantern-shaped design is all cool.

gather

⅛ yard (11.4 cm) of wool-blend felt,
    for the inner earring

⅛ yard (11.4 cm) of wool-blend felt,
    for the outer earring

⅛ yard (11.4 cm) of heavy-duty interfacing

Heavy paper

1 piece of 3mm-thick foam core, 8 x 11 inches
    (20.3 x 27.9 cm)

1 small piece of white foam board

Craft glue

Metallic acrylic paint, 2-ounce (56.7 g) tube

Textile medium, 2-ounce (56.7 g) tube

Mini eyelets designed for paper crafting

2 jump rings, 7mm

2 jump rings, 5mm

2 ear wires

Basic Sewing Kit (page 17)

Foam cutter

Mixing tray or plate for paint

Foam brush, 1 inch (2.5 cm) round

Large safety pin

Eyelet-setting tool and hammer

Jewelry pliers

Fray retardant

No specific seam allowances

make

1 Copy the templates on page 116 onto heavy paper. Set the teardrop-shaped stamp designs aside. Cut the fabrics to the following measurements:

Inner earring felt: 2 pieces 2½ inches (6.4 cm) square

Outer earring felt: 2 pieces 4 x 3 inches (10.2 x 7.6 cm) and 2 pieces using the outer earring template, placed on the fabric fold as indicated

Interfacing: 2 pieces 2½ inches (6.4 cm) square

Stamp

1 Copy the stamp designs onto the 3-mm foam core and cut them out. Cut a 6-inch (15.2 cm) square of foam board. Arrange and glue the teardrop foam shapes onto the foam board in any configuration you like. Allow the glue to dry for 20 to 25 minutes. To make handling the stamp easier, trim away any excess foam board.

2 Squeeze a liberal amount of paint onto your mixing tray. Add textile medium, using a 3:1 ratio. Brush the mixture onto the stamp. (You don't need to load it up with paint—just blot it on. If you notice little bubbles, don't worry.) Before stamping on the felt, stamp on scrap fabric or a paper towel a couple of times so the paint will stick to the stamp better.

3 Blot more paint on the stamp and stamp the design once on each of the inner earring felt squares. Let the paint dry for a few minutes, then heat set it by turning the iron on to a warm setting with no steam and press on the unstamped side of the felt.

Assemble

1 Place each inner earring piece, stamped side up, on a square of interfacing, lining up the edges.

2 Arrange each outer earring piece over an inner earring square until you like the stamped design that you see in the "window." Make sure there's at least 1/4 inch (6 mm) of the inner earring fabric extending beyond the outer earring piece so it's easier to sew.

3 Carefully sew the three layers together around the "window" opening, close to the edge of the felt, as shown in figure 1. Add a second line of stitching close to the first.

4 Turn each earring front over and cut the extra interfacing and printed felt away from the outer earring piece, leaving about 1/8 to 1/4 inch (3 to 6 mm) beyond the stitching to make sure you don't cut the seams.

5 Place each earring front in the middle of an earring back. Carefully stitch around the outer edges of the earrings. Trim off the excess earring back fabric (figure 2).

6 Use the safety pin to poke a hole 1/4 inch (6 mm) from the top of each earring. Wiggle it around a bit to make the hole slightly larger. On the right side of each earring, press the top part of the eyelet through the pinhole. The fit should be tight; you may need to use your fingernails to slip the eyelet through. If you can't get it in, use scissors to snip a tiny bit of the fabric at the pinhole.

7 Flip each earring over and slip the bottom of the eyelet onto the protruding front of the eyelet. Follow the manufacturer's instructions to set the eyelet. Make sure the eyelet is properly set by shaking the earring. There should be no movement.

8 Use pliers to attach one of the larger jump rings through each eyelet. Then attach the smaller jump ring to the larger jump ring. Finally, attach the ear wire to the small jump ring.

9 Stiffen the outer edges of the earrings by applying a small bit of fray retardant around them. Let them dry for just a few minutes and you're ready to rock your new jewelry.

figure 1

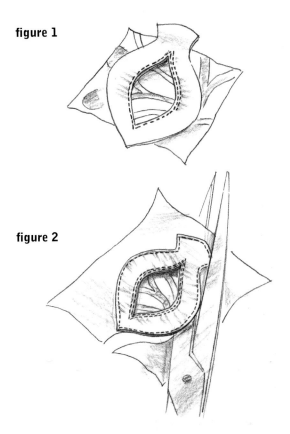

figure 2

Designer: **Rachel Fields**

Don't you love muffs? They're so quirky and old-fashioned.
Check out the scarlet lining on this black-and-white number.

gather

3 old wool sweaters of varying colors
and textures

½ yard (45.7 cm) of lining fabric

5 buttons

Embroidery floss

Basic Sewing Kit (page 17)

Seam allowance ¼ inch (6 mm)
unless otherwise noted

figure 1

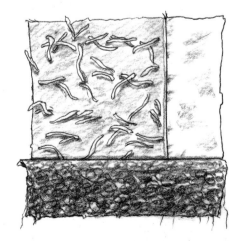

make

Cut

1 Cut the sleeves off the sweaters and set them aside.
Cut the sweaters apart at the side seams so you can use
the torsos to cut fabric squares. The muff shown was
made from three sweaters: black, white, and gray. The
gray sweater had decorative surface threads, and for
added interest, both the right and the wrong sides were
featured.

2 Cut the following pieces:

Fabric A (or gray): 12 squares, each 3½ x 3½ inches
(8.9 x 8.9 cm)

Fabric B (or black): 12 rectangles, each 1½ x 4½ inches
(3.8 x 11.4 cm)

Fabric C (or white): 12 rectangle, each 1½ x 3½ inches
(3.8 x 8.9 cm)

Assemble

1 With right sides together, sew fabric A to one long
side of fabric C.

2 With right sides together, sew the newly joined A
and C pieces to one long side of piece B (figure 1). Repeat with all the remaining pieces until you have a total
of twelve 4½-inch (11.4 cm) squares.

3 Randomly sew the squares together to make a patchwork piece that's three squares wide by four squares long.

4 Choose any three of the sweater sleeves to use inside the muff. They should be about the same size as the patchwork piece. Be sure to cut off the narrow, lower edge of the sleeve; you'll want to use the wider middle part. Stuff one cut-off sleeve into the other to make one fluffy tube. Baste the tube of sleeves to the wrong side of the quilted piece around all the edges.

5 With the right sides together, sew across the width of the patchwork piece (including the sweaters in the seam) to form a tube.

6 Cut a piece of lining fabric 12½ x 16½ inches (31.8 x 41.9 cm). With right sides together, sew the short ends to form a tube. Slide the lining tube over the quilted tube with right sides together and seams aligned. Sew one side. Press the other side of the lining and the other side of the patchwork piece ¼ inch (6 mm) to the wrong side. Flip the lining inside the tube and slipstitch the folded edges together to form the muff.

7 Instead of being quilted, this muff gets tied. Working from the outside, randomly sew the buttons to the outside of the muff with embroidery floss, catching the inner layers. Leave the tails of the embroidery floss long and tie them into a knot so they look like tassels.

Designer: **Joan K. Morris**

This quilted belt is loosely modeled on the obi,
the wide sash that holds a kimono closed.

gather

¼ yard (22.9 cm) each of three complementary
 wool fabrics for patchwork pieces
¾ yard (68.6 cm) of printed cotton for
 patchwork pieces, backing, ties, and binding
Batting, 6 x 36 inches (15.2 cm x 90 cm)
Invisible thread
Antique brass eyelet, ½ inch (1.3 cm)
 in diameter
Basic Sewing Kit (page 17)
Eyelet setter
Seam allowance ¼ inch (6 mm)
 unless otherwise noted

Note: This belt fits a waist 22 to 34 inches (55.9 to 86.4
cm), depending on the placement of the eyelet. Adjust
to fit as desired.

make

Cut

1 Cut five rectangles, each 2½ x 6 inches (6.4 x 15.2
cm), from each of the wool fabrics.

2 Cut the following pieces from the printed cotton:

5 pieces 2½ x 6 inches (6.4 x 15.2 cm), for the front

1 piece 6 x 36 inches (15.2 cm x 90 cm), for the back

2 pieces 1 x 36 inches (2.5 cm x 90 cm), for the ties

2 pieces 2 x 6 inches (5.1 x 15.2 cm), for the side edges

2 pieces 2 x 36 inches (5.1 cm x 90 cm), for the top and
bottom edges

figure 1

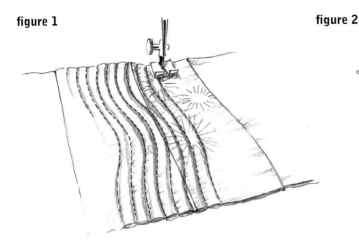

figure 2

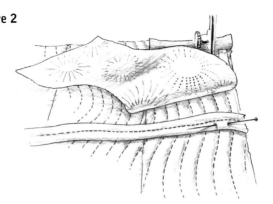

Assemble and Quilt

1 Machine stitch the long edges of the 2½ x 6-inch (6.4 x 15.2 cm) pieces with the right sides together, alternating the colors, until you have 18 pieces sewn together. You'll have two leftover pieces, which you can add if you want to make the belt longer. Press the seams open.

2 Lay out the printed cotton back piece with the wrong side up. Place the batting over it, and then add the wrong side of the finished top piece to make a quilt sandwich. Pin the layers together around the edges and through the center.

3 Using invisible thread in the needle of the sewing machine and colored thread in the bobbin, stitch in the ditch (page 24) along all the seams, through all the layers, starting in the center and working out toward both edges. Check the bottom fabric periodically to make sure it doesn't bunch.

4 Using the edge of the presser foot as a guide, machine stitch curvy lines, about ¼ inch (6 mm) apart on each of the front pieces, as shown in figure 1.

5 Machine stitch a line across the center of the belt from one short end to the other.

Ties

1 Press each of the two tie pieces in half lengthwise with the wrong sides together. Open them and press both long edges in toward the center fold. Fold the ties in half again so the pressed edges align to make each strip ¼ inch (6 mm) wide. Machine stitch close to the folded edges.

2 Pin one end of each tie to the right side at each end of the belt, with the right sides together, as shown in figure 2. Pin the side pieces to the short ends of the belt, with the right sides together and the ties caught between them. Sew the layers together using a ½-inch (1.3 cm) seam allowance.

3 Press the seams and then fold the side pieces to the back of the belt, extending the ties out from the seam. Press the unstitched edges of the side pieces ½ inch (1.3 cm) to the wrong side and then machine stitch the side pieces, through all the layers, in place to enclose the seams.

Finish

1 Center and pin the top and bottom edge strips to the long sides of the belt with the right sides together. The strips will extend beyond the ends of the belt. Stitch, using a ⅝-inch (1.6 cm) seam allowance, and press.

2 Press the extending ends of the top and bottom strips to the wrong side. Press the long unstitched edges ½ inch (1.3 cm) to the wrong side of each strip (figure 3).

3 Press the strips over the seam to the wrong side to enclose the seams. Slipstitch (page 22) the folded edges to the back of the belt.

4 For a 30-inch (76.2 cm) waist, measure in 6 inches (15.2 cm) from one end of the belt and mark the center of the belt at that point. (Adjust as desired. For a larger waist, place the eyelet closer to the end; for a smaller waist, place the eyelet farther from the end.) Set the eyelet, following the instructions on the eyelet kit. If you prefer, make a small buttonhole instead of setting an eyelet.

5 To wear the belt, center its front along the front of your body. Thread the tie end farthest from the eyelet through the eyelet and bring it to the front of your body. Bring the remaining tie end to the front too, and tie them into a bow. Cut the tie ends to the desired length. Make single knots at the end of each tie so they don't come unstitched.

figure 3

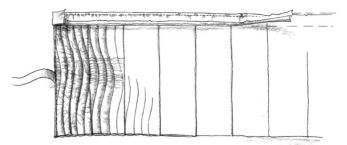

Designer: **Joan K. Morris**

Throw a jaunty cape over your shoulders, and you look pulled together, casually glamorous. A sophisticated allover quilting pattern creates a terrific texture.

gather

1 yard (90 cm) of gray wool, for the exterior
of the capelet

1 yard (90 cm) of plaid wool, for the lining

⅛ yard (11.4 cm) of cotton print,
for the appliqués

¼ yard (22.9 cm) of fusible interfacing

Invisible thread

2 skeins of embroidery floss

2 buttons, 1 ⅜ inches (3.5 cm) in diameter

Basic Sewing Kit (page 17)

Quilt-basting spray

Embroidery needle

Seam allowance ⅝ inch (1.6 cm)
unless otherwise noted

figure 1

make

Cut

1 The templates on pages 122–123 are sized for Small, Medium, and Large. Choose the size you want to make based on your usual sweater size; enlarge and cut out the appropriate templates and use them to cut the fabric as follows.

Gray wool: 2 fronts, 1 back, 2 facings, and 2 collars

Plaid wool: 1 back, 2 fronts (for the lining), and 8 large circles

Cotton print: 8 small circles

Fusible interfacing: 1 collar

2 Using the fabric marking pen or tailor's chalk, copy the matching and placement markings from the templates onto the fabric.

Assemble

1 With the right sides together, pin and stitch the front pieces to the back piece at the shoulders and overarm edges. Press the seams open. Staystitch (page 22) the neck edge.

2 Center the small circles inside the large ones, holding them in place temporarily with quilt-basting spray. Zig-zag around the edge of the smaller circle with invisible thread in the needle and colored thread in the bobbin.

3 Position the circles on the capelet so that they're evenly spaced and 4 inches (10.2 cm) from the bottom edge. Hold them in place with quilt-basting spray.

Zigzag them to the capelet with invisible thread in the needle and colored thread in the bobbin.

4 Use embroidery floss and an embroidery needle to blanket stitch around the edge of all the large circles (see figure 1 on page 74).

5 Fuse the interfacing to the wrong side of one collar piece following the manufacturer's instructions. Pin the two collar pieces right sides together and machine stitch along the sides and outside edge, leaving the neck edge open. Clip the curves and trim the seam allowance; turn the collar right side out and press. Baste the neck edges together.

Designer: **Alice Bernardo**

Amp up the coziness of a pint-sized quilt by backing it with the softest cashmere.

gather

- 1 yard (91.4 cm) of wool/cashmere blend, for quilt back
- 1 yard (91.4 cm) of fabric, for quilt front strips, quilt back strips, and hood (Fabric C)
- 7 different fabrics, ¼ yard (22.9 cm) each, for the quilt top (Fabrics A, B, and D through H)
- ¼ yard (22.9 cm) of cotton fabric, for binding
- 100% cotton batting, 32¼ inches (82 cm) square
- Heavy wool thread or yarn
- 2½ inches (6.4 cm) of brown velvet ribbon, ¾ inch (1.9 cm) wide
- Basic Sewing Kit (page 17)
- 30 safety pins
- Large embroidery needle

Finished Measurements

31½ inches (80.1 cm) square

Seam allowance ¼ inch (6 mm) unless otherwise noted

make

Cut

1 For the front of the quilt, refer to the schematic (figure 1) and cut the following strips.

Fabrics A, B, C, D, and E: Cut one strip 31½ x 3½ inches (80 x 8.9 cm) and one strip 16½ x 3½ inches (41.9 x 8.9 cm). If you're using a striped fabric, cut the shorter strip on the bias for a novelty stripe pattern.

Fabrics F and G: Cut two strips 16½ x 3½ inches (41.9 x 8.9 cm).

Fabric H: Cut one strip 16½ x 3½ inches (41.9 x 8.9 cm).

2 For the back of the quilt, refer to the schematic (figure 2) and cut the following pieces.

Fabric C: Make two strips 31½ x 2½ inches (80 x 6.4 cm), and two strips 27½ x 2½ inches (69.9 x 6.4 cm).

Wool/cashmere blend: Cut a square with sides 27½ inches (69.9 cm) long.

3 For the hood, cut two 12-inch (30.5 cm) squares, one from the wool/cashmere and one from Fabric C. Cut each square in half diagonally to make two tri-angles. Discard one of each triangle.

4 For the binding, cut enough strips 2½ inches (6.4 cm) wide to make one continuous strip approximately 14 feet (4.3 m) long (page 27).

Piece

1 For the front, lay out the five long strips, following figure 1. Sew them with right sides together. Do the same with the 10 shorter strips. Then sew the pieced units with right sides together, as shown in the schematic. Press each seam allowance toward the darker fabric to avoid show-through.

2 For the back, refer to figure 2 and sew the shorter fabric C strips to two opposite sides of the wool square with the right sides together. Press the seams toward the center. Sew the two longer strips on the remaining sides of the square, with right sides together; they are long enough to span across the wool square and the two newly attached strips of fabric C. Press these seams toward the center.

3 For the hood, sew the wool triangle and the cotton triangle with the right sides together along only the diagonal edge. Don't sew the other two sides yet. Turn the hood right side out and press lightly.

4 Place the back of the quilt face down on a flat surface. Lay the cotton batting on top and then place the wrong side of the quilt front on the batting. Smooth the layers so the edges align. Secure the layers with safety pins (page 27).

Quilt

1 Cut a piece of thread or yarn about 39 inches (1 m) long. Thread it and knot the end. To hide the knot, insert the needle into the batting and then up onto the front of the quilt. Make a second knot on the top of the quilt, near the edge so it will be hidden in the binding.

2 Quilt a straight line, with long and relaxed stitches through the center of the strips, as shown in the schematic. This will form a grid. Don't quilt the strips closest to each side. When you reach the end of the quilt side, make another knot just like the one you made to start the stitching. Remove the safety pins.

figure 2

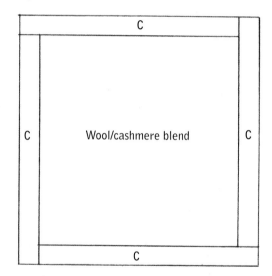

figure 1

These strips, 31½ x 3½ inches (80 x 8.9 cm)

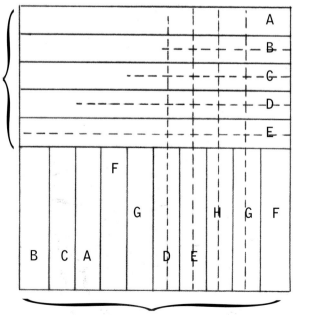

These strips, 16½ x 3½ inches (41.9 x 8.9 cm)

figure 3

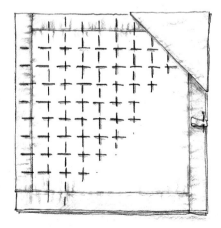

Finish

1 Pin the hood onto one of the back corners, with the wool side facing down. Sew the sides of the quilt and the hood together, leaving the diagonal edge of the hood free.

2 Fold the velvet ribbon in half, wrong sides together, and sew the raw ends to the center of one of the sides of the quilt, near the hood (figure 3).

3 To round the corners, draw a circle with a diameter of 5½ inches (14 cm) on a piece of paper. Cut it out. Place it on top of each corner of the quilt and trace it with a fabric pencil. Stitch just inside the markings. Cut all the layers at the markings.

4 Refer to page 25 to make single-fold bias binding, piecing the strips as necessary. Follow the instructions for continuous binding on page 27 to do steps 1, 2, 5, and 6, but skip the steps that miter the binding at the corners. Instead, ease the binding around the curves and be sure to catch the hood and ribbon loop in the seam. Make sure that when you slipstitch (page 22) the binding it covers the closest line of stitching.

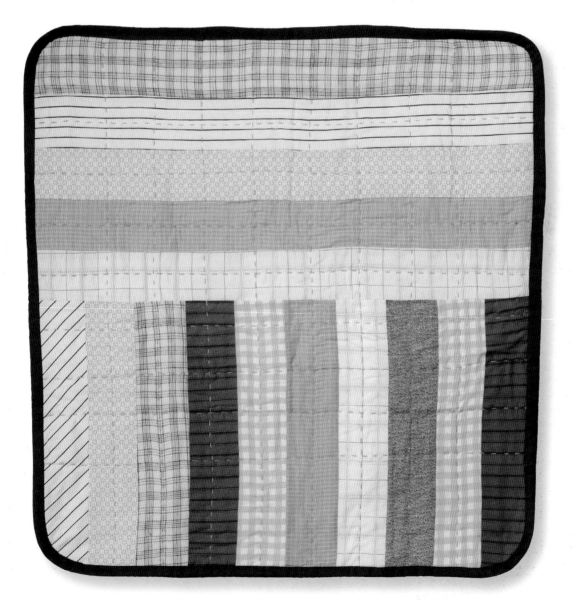

live

16

A trio of birds dangles from a wooden hoop to make a fanciful mobile. Made from herringbone wool and batik cotton, they have quilted wings and tails, and plump bellies embellished with yarn and ribbon.

gather

Brown or black felt, 3 x 15 inches
(7.6 x 38.1 cm), for the beaks

¼ yard (22.9 cm) of printed cotton,
for the tails and wings

¼ yard (22.9 cm) of non-stretch wool,
for the tails, wings, and upper bodies

¼ yard (22.9 cm) of felted wool,
for the bellies (see Note below)

¼ yard (22.9 cm) of thin cotton batting,
for the tails and wings

Cardstock

Assorted yarns, ribbons, strips of fabric
remnants, and wool roving
for embellishment

Polyester fiberfill

1 large and 3 small wooden beads

Wooden embroidery hoop, 9 inches
(22.9 cm) in diameter

Basic Sewing Kit (page 17)

Knitting needle or small paintbrush

Free-motion presser foot

Embroidery needle

Note: Either the upper body or the belly of each bird must be made of stretchy fabric, which you can make by felting a knitted wool sweater (page 20).

Seam allowance ¼ inch (6 mm)
unless otherwise noted

make

1 Trace the templates on page 117 onto cardstock and use them to cut the fabrics as indicated.

Felt—3 beaks

Printed cotton—3 right wings, 3 left wings, and 3 tails

Non-stretch wool—3 right wings, 3 left wings, 3 tails, and 3 upper bodies

Felted wool—3 bellies

Cotton batting—3 right wings, 3 left wings, and 3 tails

2 Repeat each of the following steps to make three finished birds. Baste a piece of cotton batting to the wrong side of each of the tails and wings cut from cotton fabric. With right sides together, pin the cotton wings and tails to the wool wings and tails. Sew around all the edges except the one that attaches to the body (it's indicated on the template). Backstitch all seams.

3 Turn the wings and tails right side out. Use the tip of a knitting needle or a small paintbrush to push out the tips of the wings and tails completely.

4 Set your sewing machine for free-motion sewing and attach a free-motion presser foot. Quilt the wings and tails with a series of back and forth lines (figure 1).

5 Embellish the bellies by stitching strips of torn fabric, ribbon, and pieces of wool roving along the length of the bodies.

6 Decide whether you want the cotton or the wool fabric (used to make the tails and wings) to appear on the same side as the bellies: whichever fabric you select will be considered the right side. Pin the right side of the tail and wings to the wrong side of the under body so the open ends of the wings and tails are ¼ inch (6 mm) inside the body (figure 2). Baste them in place.

Note: When you position the wings, make sure the longer curved side is near the head of the bird and that you attach one right and one left wing to each bird.

7 Pin the wrong side of a wool upper body to the wrong side of a belly. Edgestitch through all the layers, starting and stopping near the bird's head, so the bird is unstitched at the spot where the beak will attach.

8 Lightly stuff each bird with fiberfill; too much stuffing will give a lumpy appearance. Position the felt beak in the opening. Edgestitch the beak in place, simultaneously closing the bird (figure 3).

Assemble

1 Cut three pieces of yarn, each 1 yard (90 cm) long. Hand stitch the yarns to the center of the upper body of each bird. Double-check that the bird hangs at a nice angle; if necessary, reattach the hanging yarn at a different spot until you like the way the bird hangs. Thread a wooden bead onto the yarns to hide the thread knots.

2 Tie the birds to the embroidery hoop by wrapping each yarn equidistantly on the hoop. (You'll need to vary the lengths of the yarns to keep the mobile balanced.) Tie the remaining yarn ends together and thread a bead over the knot. Tie the remaining yarns into a hanging loop and snip off any excess.

figure 1

figure 2

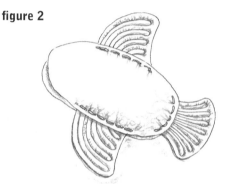

figure 3

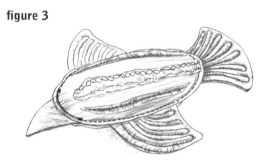

17

Designer: **Belinda Andresson**

*Punctuate the elegance of an understated cushion with a few lines
of vivid sashiko-inspired stitching, using a heavy, matte thread.*

gather

¼ yard (22.9 cm) each of four gray wools,
   for the front

¼ yard (22.9 cm) of printed cotton,
   for the front

Muslin, 13½ x 21½ inches (34.3 x 54.6 cm)

2 pieces of back fabric, each 13½ x 13 inches
   (34.3 x 33 cm)

1 skein of perle cotton (size 8) or embroidery
   floss (color to match printed fabric)

12-inch (30.5 cm) zipper

Pillow form, 13 x 20 inches (33 x 50.8 cm)

Basic Sewing Kit (page 17)

Zipper presser foot

Chopstick

Seam allowance ¼ inch (6 mm)
   unless otherwise noted

make

1 Use a rotary cutter to cut five panels for the front pillow cover to the following measurements:

2 pieces, 15 x 4 inches (38.1 x 10.2 cm)

2 pieces, 15 x 4½ inches (38.1 x 11.4 cm)

1 piece, 15 x 5 inches (38.1 x 12.7 cm)

2 Lay the five front panels out in any order. Press the muslin; it will serve as the foundation fabric.

3 Starting from the left, place the first panel right side up on the muslin so the left-hand edges of the muslin and fabric panel align. Stitch the panel to the muslin along the outer edge, backstitching at both ends (figure 1).

4 Working from left to right, position the second panel, with right sides together and right edges aligned, on top of the first panel. Stitch through all the layers, including the muslin (figure 2). Press the layers flat, and then press the second panel to the right.

5 Repeat the previous step to attach the remaining

figure 1

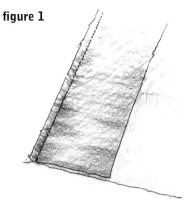

figure 2

panels so you cover the muslin.

6 Trim the wool, if necessary, to the same size as the muslin. Machine stitch the front pillow cover and muslin together around the perimeter, ¼ inch (6 mm) from the edges.

7 Using a running stitch and perle cotton or three strands of embroidery floss, hand quilt the middle three panels, stitching ¼ inch (6 mm) to the left of the seam.

8 Pin the two pillow back pieces with right sides together along the 13-inch (33 cm) edges. Install the zipper in the seam using a zipper presser foot and following the instructions for a lapped zipper on page 28.

9 With the right sides together, pin the pillow back cover to the pillow front cover with the raw edges aligned. Don't be alarmed if you have excess fabric on the sides; simply pin the pieces together and trim away any extra fabric.

10 Open the zipper. Using a ½-inch (1.3 cm) seam allowance, stitch around the perimeter of the pillow cover.

11 Serge or zigzag the raw edges. Turn the pillow cover right side out. Use a chopstick or similar tool to push the corners out. Press the cover flat and insert the pillow form. Close the zipper.

Designer: **Lindy Emser**

The hexagon is a time-honored shape for quilt blocks, but that's the only traditional aspect of this contemporary honeycombed table runner, which manages to be both funky and elegant while looking invitingly handmade.

gather

4 wool sweaters, in monochromatic color
   scheme
Wool-blend felt, 45 x 18 inches
   (114.3 x 45.7 cm)
Paper-backed fusible web, 45 x 18 inches
   (114.3 x 45.7 cm)
Basic Sewing Kit (page 17)
Template plastic or heavy cardboard
No specific seam allowance

make

Cut

1 Felt the sweaters (page 20) and dry them completely in the dryer with the heat set on high.

2 Cut the sweaters apart along the seams so you have four large pieces—a front, a back, and two sleeves—from each. Cut these pieces into strips 3½ inches (8.9 cm) wide.

3 Copy the hexagon template on page 114 onto plastic or cardboard and cut it out. Use it to trace 48 hexagon-shaped tiles onto the strips and cut them out with a rotary cutter.

Sew

1 Arrange the tiles as shown in the schematic (figure 1). To add visual interest, lay some of the tiles right side up and others right side down.

figure 1

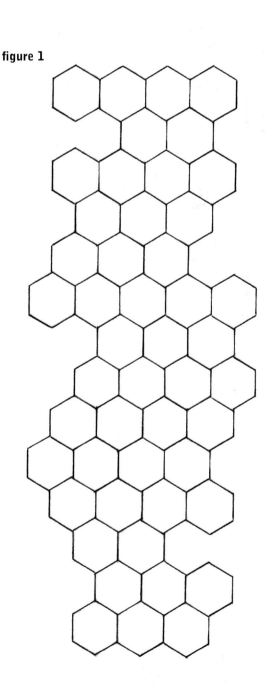

figure 2

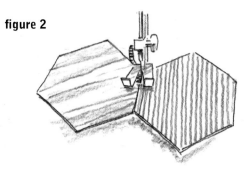

figure 3

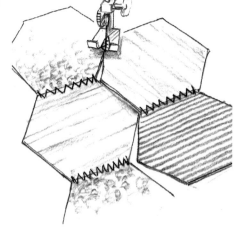

2 To stitch the tiles together, set your sewing machine for a zigzag stitch. Abut the edges of two flat tile pieces and sew them together so that the stitch catches both pieces (figure 2).

3 Make the top of the runner by joining the remaining tiles in short rows of between two and five tiles. Then sew the rows together. Pivot the piece as needed to sew the rows together smoothly and without stopping the stitching between tiles (figure 3).

4 Lay the runner on the fusible web with the paper side up and trace around the perimeter. Cut the fusible web slightly smaller than the traced marking.

5 Following the manufacturer's instructions, and with a fairly hot iron, fuse the web to the runner; try to keep any loose threads between the layers. Remove the paper backing and fuse the runner/web to the felt. Trim the felt with sharp scissors to the same size as the runner.

6 Run a straight stitch along the entire border of the runner, ⅛ inch (3 mm) from the edge.

7 Quilt the runner as desired. Here, the designer quilted only a select few tiles with a straight stitch that spirals from the outside of the hexagon toward the center. **Note:** The thickness of the runner might make it difficult to quilt designs with sharp curves, so a straight pattern is simpler to stitch.

Designer: **Tamara Erbacher**

Warm-hued wool + luxurious cotton prints = heirloom quilt

gather

21 different fabrics, cotton prints and
solid-colored wools (see yardage and
cutting chart on the facing page)

1¾ yards (1.6 m) of 40-inch (101.6 cm)
wide fabric for the backing

15 inches (38.1 cm) of 45-inch (114.3 cm)
wide fabric for the binding

Batting, 55 x 60 inches (139.7 x 152.4 cm)

Basic Sewing Kit (page 17)

Template plastic

Craft knife

Quilt-basting pins

Walking presser foot

Masking tape

Finished Measurements

40 x 56 inches (101.6 x 142.2 cm)

Seam allowance ¼ inch (6 mm)
unless otherwise noted

make

Cut

1 Trace the templates on page 119 onto the template
plastic and cut them out with a craft knife.

2 Cut the fabrics, following the chart on the facing
page. Use a rotary cutter to cut the squares, but cut any
curves with scissors.

3 Arrange the pieces as shown in figure 1.

Piece

1 To piece the squares, follow the schematic and work
with one square at a time. Fold the corresponding
outer circle and the inner circle in half and then in half
again and pin or press mark the folds. This provides
equidistant marks for matching the two pieces (see
figure 2 on page 94).

figure 1

Fabric number	Quantity to purchase	Quantity of inner circles to cut	Quantity of outer circle to cut	Quantity of 8½-inch (21.6 cm) squares to cut
1	Fat quarter	4	2	
2 and 3	Fat quarter		4	
4	Fat quarter	4		
5 and 6	Fat quarter	2	2	
7	Fat quarter		3	
8	Fat quarter	3		
9, 11, and 13	Fat eighth	2		
10 and 12	Fat eighth		2	
14 and 16	9-inch (22.9 cm) square	1		
15 and 17	9-inch (22.9 cm) square		1	
18, 19, 20, and 21	Fat quarter			3

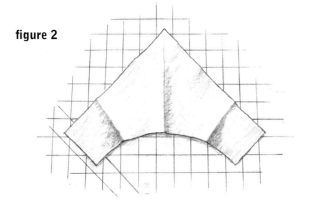

figure 2

2 With right sides together and the inner circle on top, pin the outer circle and inner circle together, matching the markings (figure 3). Use a lot of pins—more pins are better than fewer when it comes to piecing curves. Sew slowly, being careful to maintain the 1/4-inch (6 mm) seam allowance. Press the seams open, and then press the front.

3 Once all the blocks have been pieced, sew them into rows, referring to the schematic.

4 Complete the quilt top by sewing the rows together. To align the squares as accurately as possible, place a pin through the seam intersection points perpendicular to the seam you're sewing. If some of these points don't meet accurately, stretch the fabric to avoid forming tucks.

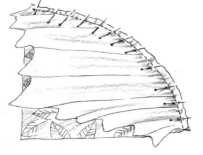

figure 3

Assemble

1 Make the quilt sandwich as described on page 23. Use basting pins to pin the quilt sandwich together, from the center out toward all the corners, keeping the pins about 3 inches (7.6 cm) apart.

2 Attach the walking presser foot to your machine, and, using the edge of the presser foot as a guide, machine stitch on each side of all of the vertical joining seams, starting in the center of the quilt and working toward each side (figure 4).

3 Trim away any excess batting. Use a ruler and rotary cutter to trim the edges of the quilt straight.

4 Press the binding fabric and cut six strips across the width of the fabric, each 2 1/2 inches (6.4 cm) wide. Piece the strips together to make one continuous binding strip (page 27), and then press the binding strip as described on page 25 to make single-fold binding.

5 To attach the binding strip to the quilt, refer to continuous binding on page 27. Be sure to use the walking presser foot and a scant 3/8-inch (1 cm) seam allowance.

6 Hand stitch the binding to the back of the quilt using a slipstitch (page 22).

figure 4

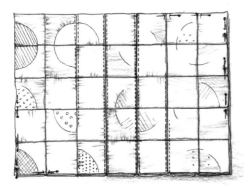

20

Designer: **Dorie Blaisdell Schwarz**

Sure, a little woolen potholder wrapped around the handle of a hot kettle can prevent accidents, but let's be honest: you'll really just want to make one because it's so dang cute.

gather

Red felted sweater remnant, 8½ x 5 inches
    (21.6 x 12.7 cm)

Cotton fabric remnant, for the backing,
    8½ x 5 inches (21.6 x 12.7 cm)

Cotton fabric remnant, for binding strips,
    1½ x 31 inches (3.8 x 78.7 cm)

Cotton fabric, for the ties, 1½ x 14 inches
    (3.8 x 35.6 cm)

1 package of ½-inch (1.3 cm) double-fold
    bias tape (optional substitute for fabric
    binding strips and tie)

1 button

Basic Sewing Kit (page 17)

Seam allowance ¼ inch (6 mm)
    unless otherwise noted

make

1 Pin the felted sweater and the cotton backing fabrics with the wrong sides together.

2 Use a disappearing ink fabric marker to mark lengthwise quilting lines. Mark the first line in the center of the pinned pieces. Mark two additional lines on either side of the first line and 1 inch (2.5 cm) apart. Machine stitch the lines, beginning with the middle line and working out toward each side.

figure 1

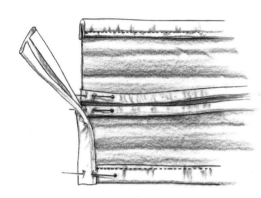

3 After quilting, the edges of the cotton might not align with the edges of the felt because wool can stretch during stitching. Trim the wool felt to make the edges even.

4 To make the binding strips and ties, press the cotton fabrics in half with the wrong sides together and make single-fold binding (page 28). Cut two 7-inch (17.8 cm) ties from the 14-inch (35.6 cm) strip. Cut the binding strips from the 31-inch (78.7 cm) strip as follows: two pieces 6 inches (15.2 cm) long and two pieces 9½ inches (24.1 cm) long.

tip

You can substitute premade bias tape for fabric binding strips. It comes in single- or double-fold and in many colors.

5 To bind the potholder, refer to topstitching binding on page 25. Before binding one short side, pin the edges of the two ties to the edge of the red wool, so you can catch them in the seam (figure 1).

6 Trim the tie ends at an angle. Wrap the potholder, felt side out, around the handle of a teapot, and mark the button location so the ties can wrap around the button to hold the potholder in place. Sew on the button.

Designer: **Rebeka Lambert**

Declare war on the cold air that slips through window cracks and below doors: just plop a quilted draft dodger on sills to help keep your pad cozy.

gather
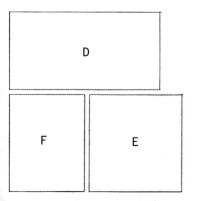

- ½ yard (45.7 cm) of brown wool
- ¼ yard (22.9 cm) each of 5 different printed fabrics
- ⅓ yard (30.5 cm) of batting
- Basic Sewing Kit (page 17)
- Safety pins
- 10 pounds (4.5 kg) of dried beans or rice (optional)
- Seam allowance ¼ inch (6 mm) unless otherwise noted

make

Cut

1 Use the rotary cutter to cut the following fabrics. Using a disappearing ink fabric marker, label the pieces with the appropriate letter.

Cut 18 pieces of wool to the following measurements:

8 pieces, 4 x 3½ inches (10.2 x 8.9 cm) (A)
8 pieces, 4 x 6 inches (10.2 x 15.2 cm) (B)
2 pieces, 6 x 12½ inches (15.2 x 31.8 cm) (C)

figure 1

figure 2

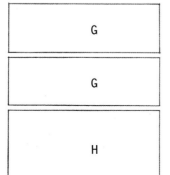

Cut 24 pieces of the printed fabrics, in a random assortment, to the following measurements:

Block #1

4 pieces, 4 x 2 inches (10.2 x 5.1 cm) (D)
4 pieces, 2½ x 2½ inches (6.4 x 6.4 cm) (E)
4 pieces, 2½ x 2 inches (6.4 x 5.1 cm) (F)

Block #2

8 pieces, 1¼ x 4 inches (3.2 x 10.2 cm) (G)
4 pieces, 2 x 4 inches (5.1 x 10.2 cm) (H)

Piece

1 Assemble and sew four blocks using #1 block pieces (with the right sides together), as shown in figure 1.

2 Assemble and sew four blocks using #2 block pieces (with the right sides together), as shown in figure 2.

3 Create eight strips by sewing one A and one B wool piece to either side of each of the patterned blocks (with the right sides together), as shown in the schematic (see figure 3 on page 100), rotating the blocks for a random appearance.

4 Sew the strips with the right sides together to create one large piece.

5 Sew the two remaining large pieces of wool to what you've already assembled, with the right sides together, one on each end.

Quilt

1 Cut a piece of batting slightly larger than the pieced work. Secure the batting to the wrong side of the pieced dodger with safety pins. Machine quilt the layers together using any design you like. See pages 23–24 for suitable quilting techniques.

figure 3

		A				A		B			A		B		A
B					B								D		G
		G	G	H		G	G	H							G
F					F				H		F	E		E	F	H
E	D				E	D		G							
								G					D		
		B				B				B				B
A					A			A			A			

2 Fold the quilted piece in half lengthwise with the right sides together. Using a ½-inch (1.3 cm) seam allowance, create a tube by sewing the long side, leaving a 6-inch (15.2 cm) opening at the center.

3 Fold one end of the tube in half, with right sides together, so it's closed. Stitch ½ inch (1.3 cm) from one fold toward the center for about 1 inch (2.5 cm), then backstitch. Repeat from the opposite fold, leaving the center unstitched. Fold the tube so the seams you just sewed meet in the center and the unstitched portions are on the sides. Stitch from the sides, ending at the center, to form a shape that looks like a plus sign (figure 4). This closes off the end of the tube. Repeat on the other end of the tube.

4 Turn the tube right side out. If you want, make it heavier by filling it with dried rice or beans. Slipstitch (page 22) the opening shut.

figure 4

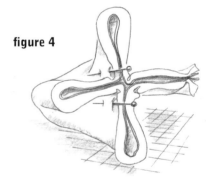

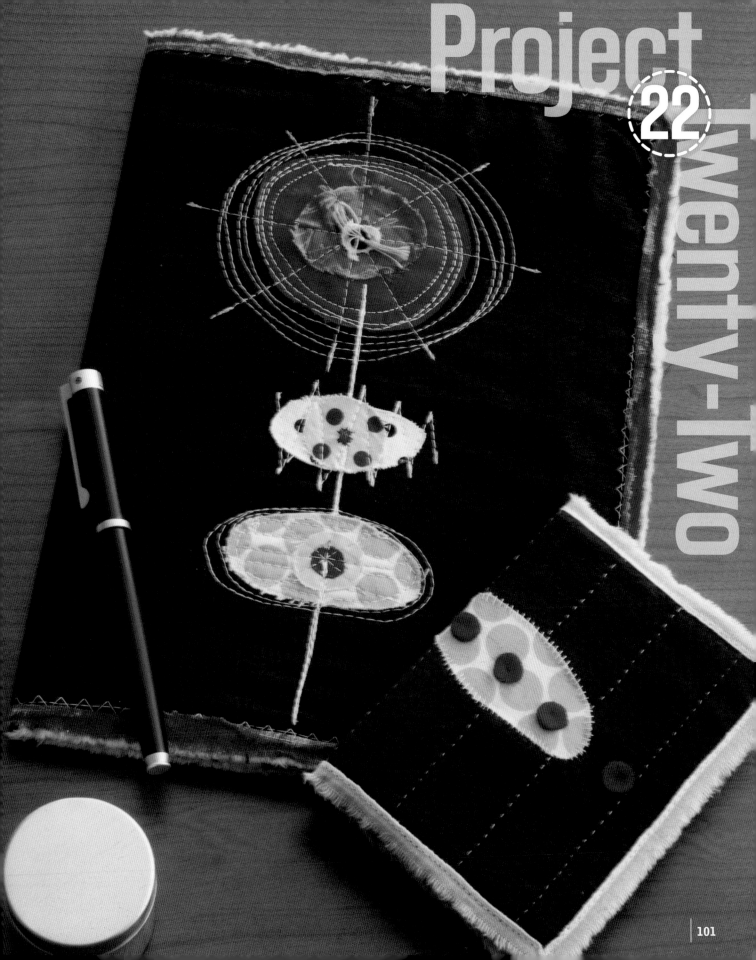

22

Designer: **Margaret Couch Cogswell**

Camouflage a boring old composition book with a sweet little stitched cover, and you'll be too cool for school.

gather

1 pair of old, recycled men's wool pants

½ yard (45.7 cm) of cotton fabric or
    recycled garment

1 square of felt

Scraps of cotton fabric or old garments

Composition notebook

Scrap paper

Thread in matching and contrasting colors
    to fabrics

1 yard (90 cm) of embroidery floss

Basic Sewing Kit (page 17)

Embroidery needle

No specific seam allowance

make

Cut

1 Create a pattern for the cover. Open the composition book to the middle, lay it flat, and record its exact measurements. Add ¾ inch (1.9 cm) to the length and width measurements to allow for the bulk of layering fabric and the seam allowance. On the scrap paper, draw a rectangle of the appropriate size and cut it out. This is the pattern for the cover.

2 Create a pattern for the inside panel. To determine the length, measure from the top to the bottom of the composition book and add ¾ inch (1.9 cm) for bulk and seam allowance. The width of the pattern piece will be 4¾ inches (12 cm) for a large composition book, or 2¼ inches (5.7 cm) for a small one. Draw a rectangle of the appropriate size and cut it out.

3 Using the paper patterns, cut one cover and two inside panels from the wool pants.

4 Tear or cut out two covers (one of which will serve as the middle layer, described later) and two inside panels from the cotton fabric. If you tear the fabric, remove all the hanging threads from the cloth so it won't keep unraveling.

5 Cut out ten or more circular and oval shapes from the felt and fabric scraps in a variety of sizes. You'll layer the shapes on the cover, so make them as large as 3 inches (7.6 cm) and as small as ½ inch (1.3 cm) in diameter.

Assemble

1 The cover consists of three layers of fabric: the outside cover (wool), the inside cover (cotton), and a middle layer (cotton), which isn't visible but adds stability. Pin the outside and inside covers with wrong sides together and the middle layer sandwiched between them. Zigzag along the edges.

2 Make a quilted pattern, like on the small notebook cover, by straight stitching (by hand) vertical, parallel lines 1 inch (2.5 cm) apart on the front of the cover.

3 Arrange and pin the shapes on the cover any way you like, referring to the photograph for inspiration. Machine and/or hand sew along the raw edges and through all the fabric layers, so the shapes don't unravel.

4 Further embellish the cover with embroidery floss, and/or decorative topstitching over, around, and through the shapes.

5 Pin one wool inside panel and one cotton inside panel, wrong sides together. Zigzag around all the edges. Repeat with the remaining inside panel pieces.

6 Make a pocket for one of the inside panels by tearing a 3 x 6-inch (7.6 x 15.2 cm) rectangle from a cotton scrap. Fold it in half, wrong sides together, to create a square. Zigzag the three raw edges and embellish one side with a fabric circle appliqué and decorative stitching. Pin the pocket near the bottom of one of the panels with the embellished side up and zigzag or hand stitch it in place around the sides and bottom.

7 To make the trim, tear cotton strips ¼ to ⅜ inch (6 mm to 1 cm) wide. Remove any hanging threads. Adjust your sewing machine so the zigzag stitch is almost as wide as the trim; this will allow you to stitch in the center of the trim, leaving a bit of fabric loose on each side to create a slightly frayed look. Zigzag the strips to the inside edge of the interior panels to finish the edges.

8 With wrong sides together, pin an interior panel to the right and the left side of the cover. Zigzag the panels to the cover along the three outside edges of the panels (figure 1).

9 Tear more cotton fabric strips to make trim for the exterior of the notebook jacket. You can use a single strip or make one from a combination of fabrics. Zigzag it to the perimeter of the cover, overlapping the edges on the back of the cover. Ease the trim around the corners, or fold it into a miter (page 27).

figure 1

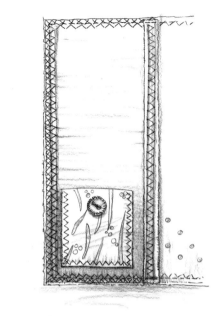

Give an old footstool new life with a natty cover-up.
An embroidered design doubles as quilting.

gather

Wool to amply cover width and length of stool

Muslin, same size as batting

Stool

Batting to fit quilting template plus 2 inches
(5.1 cm) in each direction

Quilting thread, carpet thread, or heavy-gauge
silk thread

Trim, amount equal to bottom perimeter of
cover plus 2 inches (5.1 cm)

Button

Basic Sewing Kit (page 17)

Commercial quilting template

No specific seam allowance

make

Cut

1 Measure the top of the stool. Add the desired skirt
length, plus ½ inch (1.3 cm) for the hem, to each side.
Cut the wool to these dimensions. Zigzag the edges of
the wool to reduce fraying.

example

Stool top dimensions are	*17 x 15 inches (43.2 x 38.1 cm)*
Desired skirt length is	*3½ inches (8.9 cm) on each side*
Hem allowance is	*½ inch (1.3 cm) on each side*
Fabric cutting dimensions are	*25 x 23 inches (63.5 x 58.4 cm)*

figure 1

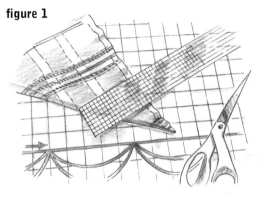

2 Trace the quilting template onto the center front
of the wool with a disappearing marker. Measure the
quilting template and add 2 inches (5.1 cm) to the measurements in each direction. Cut both the muslin and
the batting to this size.

3 Center and pin the batting and then the muslin to the
wrong side of the stool fabric, so they're directly under
the traced design. Baste them in place. Hand quilt the
design with a straight stitch and heavy thread. Remove
the basting stitches and trim the batting and the muslin
to within 1 inch (2.5 cm) of the quilted design.

4 Fold the edges of one corner with right sides together
to form a triangle (figure 1). Measure from the triangle
point and make a mark at the desired skirt length plus
hem allowance on the fabric edge. With tailor's chalk
draw a line perpendicular to the edge at the marking.
Stitch across the line; backstitch at both ends of the
stitching. Trim away the excess fabric. Repeat on the
remaining three corners.

5 Press the hem edge to the wrong side and pin the fold
to the top edge of the trim. Edgestitch the trim to the
bottom of the stool cover.

6 Sew the button in the center of the quilted design.

Designer: **Lindy Emser**

What makes this toss pillow so appealing—the traditional tile pattern that escapes convention by not covering the entire front? The fuzzy felted fabric in warm, soft tones? The cozy way it feels when you hug it? It's a toss-up.

gather

1 gray wool sweater

1 teal wool sweater

1 white wool sweater

⅔ yard (61 cm) of houndstooth fabric, for the back

1 yard (90 cm) of fusible interfacing

Zipper, 16 inches (40.6 cm) long

Foam pillow form, 18 inches (45.7 cm) square

Basic Sewing Kit (page 17)

Template plastic or heavy cardboard

Zipper presser foot

Seam allowance ½ inch (1.3 cm) unless otherwise noted

make

Cut

1 Felt the sweaters (page 20) and dry them completely in the dryer set on high heat.

2 Cut the sweaters apart along all the seams so you end up with four large pieces—a front, a back, and two sleeves—for each one.

3 For the background of the pillow front, cut an 18-inch (45.7 cm) square from the gray felted sweater. If you don't have a large enough piece, sew two pieces together. Don't worry about a seam; it will either be covered up or add an interesting visual element to the background.

4 To cut the 23 teal octagons, slice the teal felted sweater into strips 3 inches (7.6 cm) wide. Further cut the strips into 3-inch (7.6 cm) squares. Copy the octagon template on page 114 onto plastic or cardboard and cut it out. Use it to trim the corners off the squares and create the octagonal tiles.

5 To cut the 20 square tiles from the white felted sweater, cut strips 1 inch (2.5 cm) wide, then cut those into 1-inch (2.5 cm) squares.

Assemble

1 Lay out the design for the pillow front as shown in the schematic. You can lay some of the tiles right side up and others right side down to add visual interest (figure 1).

2 Set your sewing machine for a zigzag stitch. You'll sew the octagons and squares together before sewing them to the background fabric. To do so, abut the edges of two octagons and sew them together so the stitch catches both pieces. Sew the octagons into strips as follows:

2 strips of 2 octagons
3 strips of 4 octagons
1 strip of 5 octagons
2 single octagons

3 Referring to the schematic, sew the strips together while adding the small squares. To do this, position two strips together and sew the first octagons in those strips with the edges abutted as in step 2. As you come to the end of the abutting edges of the first two octagons, stop stitching and position a white square in the opening between the two octagons. Pivot the needle to sew the square to the octagon. Sew one side of the square, pivot again, and sew the second side. Then, sew the edges of the next two octagons in the strip together (figure 2). Continue in the same manner to finish joining the octagonal strips.

figure 2

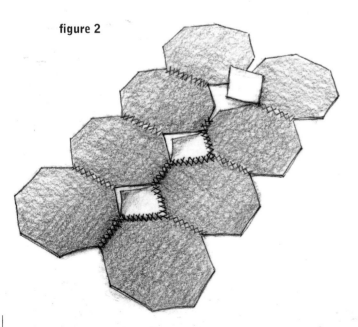

4 To complete the joining of the two strips, zigzag stitch the two unstitched sides of each square. Pull any threads to the back of the work. Continue in this way until all the octagons are sewn together as shown in the schematic.

5 Lay the large and both small octagonal designs on a piece of fusible interfacing and trace around them loosely. Cut the interfacing slightly smaller than the traced line. Use a fairly hot iron and follow the manufacturer's instructions to fuse the tile designs onto the pillow front, pushing any loose threads between the layers to hide them. You'll need to trim some of the octagons to align with the edges of the pillow front.

6 Use tailor's chalk to mark intersecting lines through the center of all the connected octagons, as shown in the schematic. Machine stitch over the markings to quilt a gridlike pattern.

7 After quilting, zigzag around the perimeters with the stitch half on the gray background and half on the teal or white shapes.

8 Cut two rectangles from the pillow back fabric, one 18 x 7 inches (45.7 x 17.8 cm) and the other 18 x 14 inches (45.7 x 35.6 cm). With the right sides together, pin the two pieces with 1 ¹/₂-inch (3.8 cm) seam allowances along the 18-inch (45.7 cm) edges to make a square.

9 Install the zipper, using the zipper foot and following the instructions for a lapped zipper on page 28.

10 Open the zipper and with right sides together, sew the quilted front to the back around all four edges. Turn the pillow cover right side out, insert the pillow form, and close the zipper.

figure 1

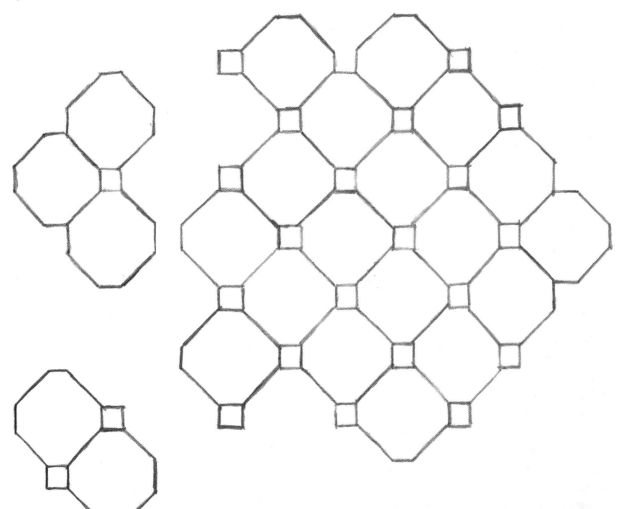

Designer: **Cheyenne Goh**

Just because you've called in sick to work doesn't mean you can't suit up. Climb back into bed and cosset yourself with a hot water bottle tucked into a cozy made from a recycled waistcoat.

gather

1 button-front tailored wool vest, with
   original buttons

Scraps of four or five different wool suitings,
   1/8 yard (11.4 cm) total

1/2 yard (45.7 cm) of gray wool fabric, for the
   lining

Batting, 15 x 9 1/2 inches (38 x 24.1 cm)

2 buttons, 3/4 inch (1.9 cm) in diameter

Basic Sewing Kit (page 17)

Zipper presser foot

Seam allowance 1/4 inch (6 mm)
   unless otherwise noted

make

Cut

1 Cut away the center front edges of the vest, 2 1/2 inches (6.4 cm) from the finished edges, so you have one strip with buttons and one with buttonholes.

2 Cut up the rest of the front of the vest, as well as the suiting scraps, into approximately 35 rectangles of varying sizes; they can be about 2 3/4 inches (7 cm) wide and between 2 and 6 inches (5.1 and 15.2 cm) long.

3 Cut the lining fabric into three pieces, each 15 x 9 1/2 inches (38 x 24.1 cm).

Back

1 Sew the short edges of two rectangles with right sides together. Continue in this way, sewing rectangles together along the short edges, to make a strip at least 15 inches (38 cm) long. The strip may end up longer than 15 inches (38 cm) because of the varied length of the rectangles, in which case simply cut off the excess fabric. Make three more strips the same way.

2 Sew the strips together lengthwise, with the right sides together, to form a patchwork piece that measures 15 x 9 1/2 inches (38 x 24.1 cm).

3 Place the patchwork, wrong side down, on the batting and stitch them together on all four sides.

4 Pin one of the lining pieces to the patchwork piece, right sides together. Stitch around all the sides, 1/4 inch (6 mm) from the edge, leaving 8 inches (20.3 cm) open on one of the shorter sides. Turn the piece right side out. Press the edges of the opening to the inside and edgestitch (page 22) the entire side, closing the opening with the stitching. Edgestitch the other short edge also.

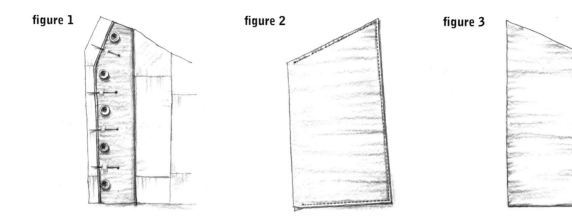

figure 1 **figure 2** **figure 3**

Inner Flap

1 Sew rectangles together as in step 1 of the back. Make four strips, each 13¾ inches (35 cm) long. Cut off any excess fabric.

2 Sew three of the four strips together lengthwise, with right sides together, to make a patchwork piece.

3 With right sides together, sew the cut edge of the button strip (cut from the front of the vest) to one long edge of the patchwork piece.

4 Position the original finished edge of the button strip over the remaining rectangle strip so the button edge is about 1⅛ inch (2.8 cm) from the left edge, covering more than half the strip. Pin, and topstitch the pieces together, as close as possible to the finished edge of the button strip (figure 1). (Switch to a zipper presser foot to make maneuvering around the buttons easier.)

5 To shape the top, orient it vertically, with the row of buttons on the left. Measure and mark 8¼ inches (21 cm) from the bottom of the opposite vertical side. Use tailor's chalk to draw a line from the top left corner to the marking on the right. Cut along the marking.

6 Pin one of the gray wool lining pieces to the patchwork piece, right sides together. Trim away the top of the lining, following the shape of the patchwork piece.

7 Machine stitch around all the sides, ¼ inch (6 mm) from the edge, leaving 8 inches (20.3 cm) open on the bottom. Turn the piece right side out. Press the edges of the opening to the inside and edgestitch (page 22) the entire side, closing the opening with the stitching. Edgestitch the top of the inner flap as well.

Outer Flap

1 Sew rectangles together as in step 1 for the back. Make three strips, each 13¾ inches (35 cm) long. Cut off any excess fabric.

2 Sew the three strips together lengthwise, right sides together, to make a patchwork piece. Orient the piece vertically. With the chalk, mark 9½ inches (24 cm) from the bottom on the left vertical side. Draw a line from the top right corner to the chalk mark and cut along the line.

3 Pin the patchwork and remaining lining pieces with right sides together and trim the top of the lining, using the patchwork piece as a guide. Machine stitch the pieces together around all the edges, except the shorter vertical side. Start and stop the stitching ¼ inch (6 mm) from the open edges (figure 2). Turn the piece right side out.

4 Lay the buttonhole strip over the buttons on the inner flap and pin mark a section at least 9½ inches (24 cm) long that aligns with the buttons and includes at least four buttonholes. If you cut away the finished top or bottom edge of the buttonhole strip, you'll need to cut the strip a little longer than the flap opening, so you can fold the cut edges of the buttonhole strip to the inside. Cut the strip at the markings and fold the top or bottom edges, if necessary, to the inside and pin them in place.

5 Manipulate the buttonhole strip so it fits the flap opening. With the right sides together, pin the cut edge of the buttonhole strip to the right side of the outer flap opening. Sew the seam.

figure 4

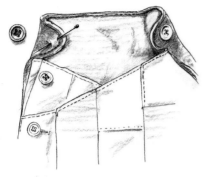

6 Fold the cut edge of the lining to the wrong side to cover the seam. Edgestitch the lining in place, as close as possible to the fold. Edgestitch around the edges of the outer flap, closing the openings—if there are any—in the top and bottom of the buttonhole strip (figure 3).

Assemble and Quilt

1 Machine quilt the back, inner flap, and outer flap pieces individually by stitching-in-the-ditch (page 24).

2 Pin the inner flap to the back piece with the lining sides together and the side and bottom edges aligned. Machine stitch the pieces together as close as possible to the sides and bottom edge.

3 Button the outer flap to the inner flap with the right side facing up and the right sides aligned. Pin and stitch the three pieces together along the right side only.

4 Fold the top corners of the back piece to the front and toward the center. Sew a button through all the fabric layers to hold each flap down (figure 4).

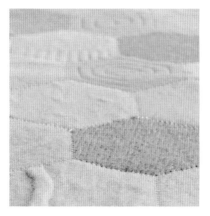

Page 88
Actual size

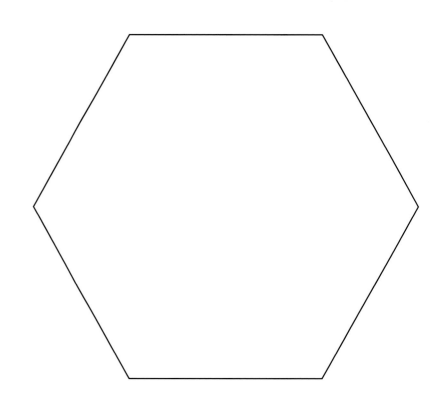

Page 106
Actual size

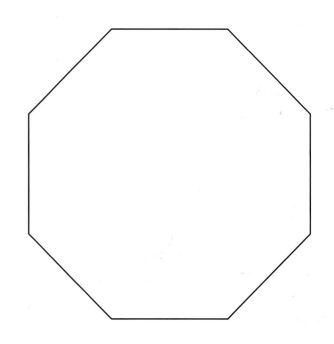

A

Bottom

Top

Side

B

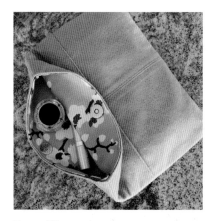

Page 47
Enlarge 200%

Page 38
Enlarge 200%

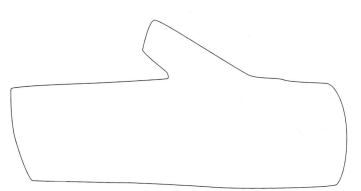

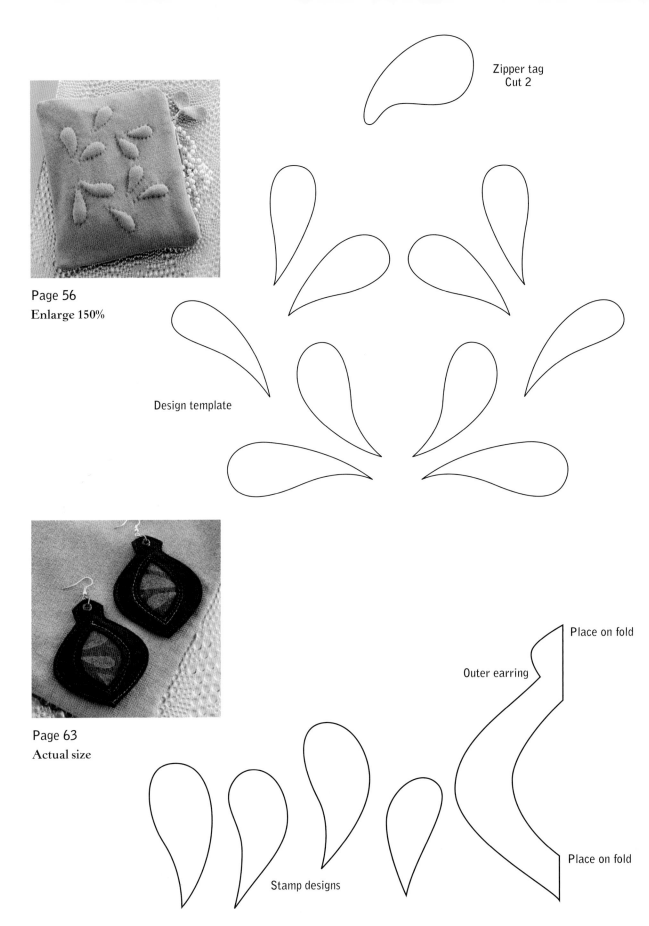

Zipper tag
Cut 2

Page 56
Enlarge 150%

Design template

Page 63
Actual size

Place on fold

Outer earring

Place on fold

Stamp designs

Tail

Don't sew along this edge

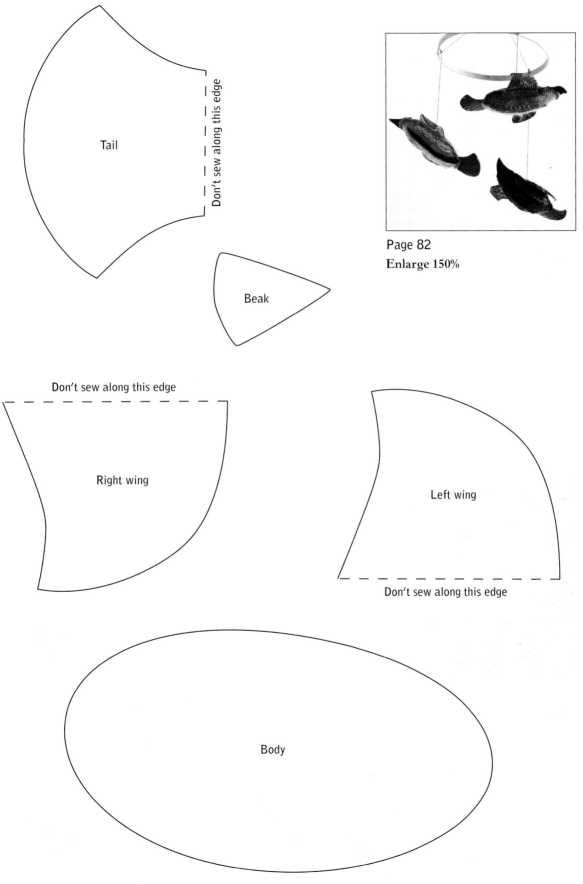

Page 82
Enlarge 150%

Beak

Don't sew along this edge

Right wing

Left wing

Don't sew along this edge

Body

Page 44
Actual size

Page 36
Enlarge 200%

Front

Cut 1 from felt and
1 from lining fabric

Back

Cut 1 from felt and
1 from lining fabric

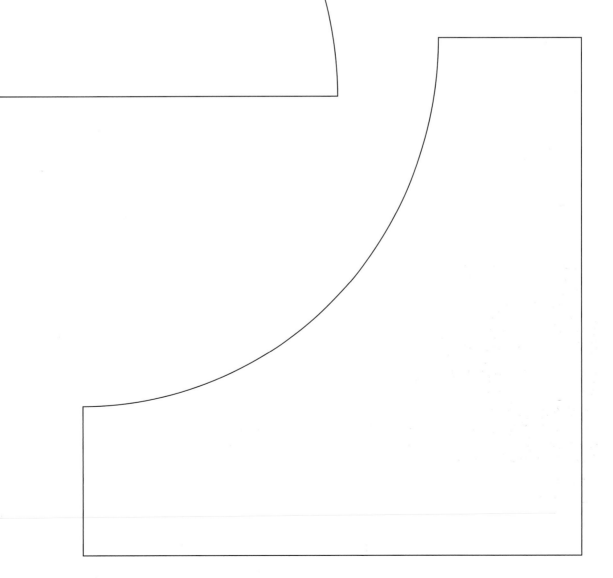

Page 91
Actual size

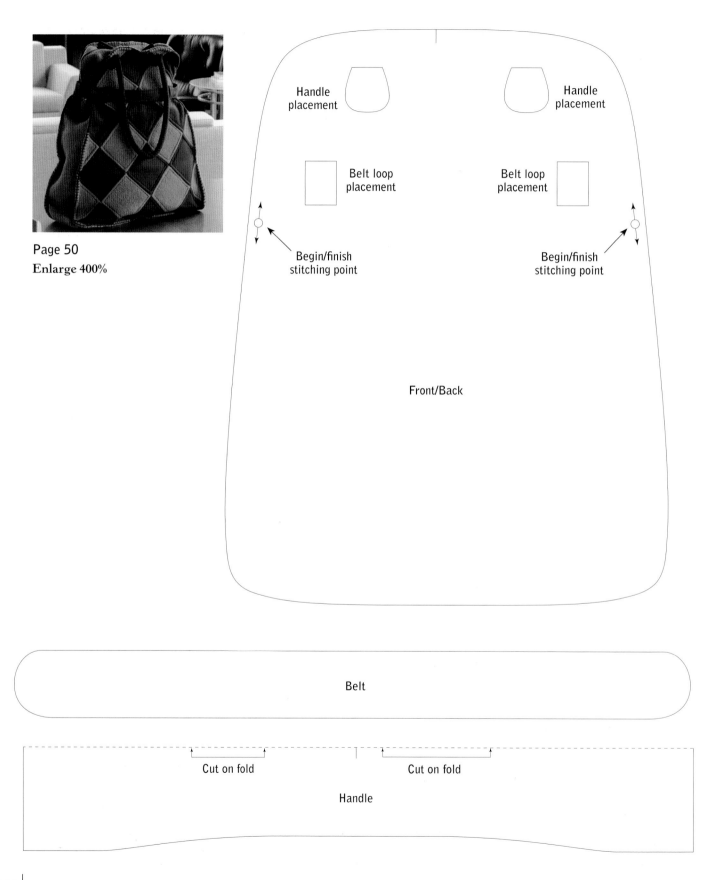

Page 50
Enlarge 400%

Handle placement

Handle placement

Belt loop placement

Belt loop placement

Begin/finish stitching point

Begin/finish stitching point

Front/Back

Belt

Cut on fold

Cut on fold

Handle

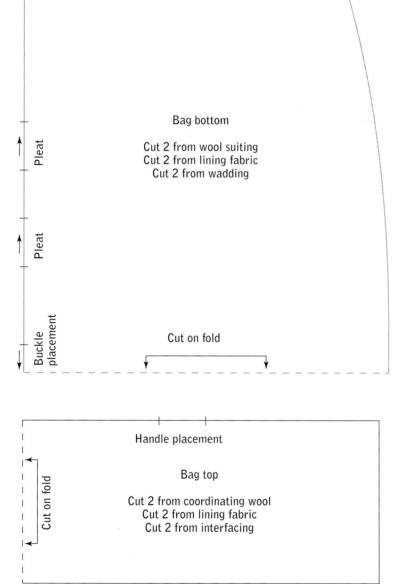

Bag bottom

Cut 2 from wool suiting
Cut 2 from lining fabric
Cut 2 from wadding

Pleat

Pleat

Buckle placement

Cut on fold

Page 32
Enlarge 200%

Handle placement

Bag top

Cut 2 from coordinating wool
Cut 2 from lining fabric
Cut 2 from interfacing

Cut on fold

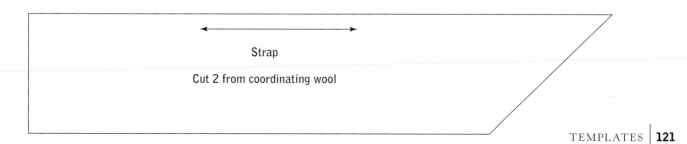

Strap

Cut 2 from coordinating wool

Page 73
Enlarge 325%

Bottom
appliqué

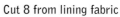

Cut 8 from lining fabric

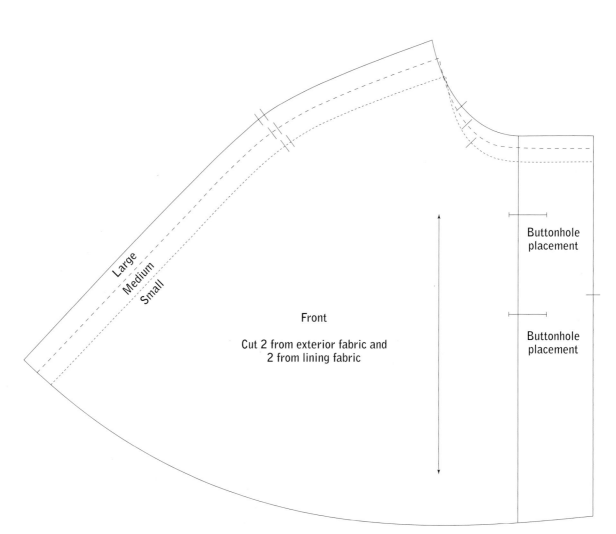

Large

Medium

Small

Buttonhole
placement

Front

Cut 2 from exterior fabric and
2 from lining fabric

Buttonhole
placement

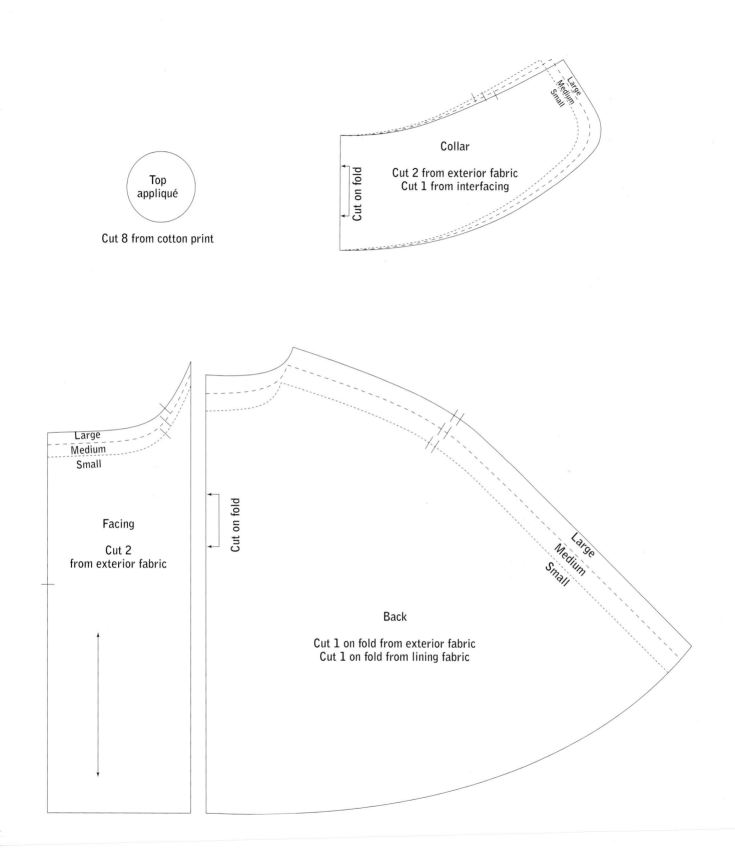

Top
appliqué

Cut 8 from cotton print

Collar

Cut 2 from exterior fabric
Cut 1 from interfacing

Cut on fold

Large
Medium
Small

Facing

Cut 2
from exterior fabric

Large
Medium
Small

Cut on fold

Back

Cut 1 on fold from exterior fabric
Cut 1 on fold from lining fabric

Large
Medium
Small

Belinda Andresson's interest in craft was sparked a few years ago after discovering numerous craft blogs online. Since then, her love of craft has gone from a passing hobby to an integral part of her everyday life. She has contributed to several Lark books, including *Pretty Little Presents* (2009), *Sweet Booties!* (2009), and *Pretty Little Patchwork* (2008). You can read more about Belinda's craft projects and family life at www.tuttifruiti.blogspot.com and tuttifruitidesigns. wordpress.com.

Robin Beaver's mother and grandmother inspired a love of needlecraft in her when she was very young, and ever since then it has served as a source of great creativity, satisfaction, and peace in her life. She enjoys sewing, knitting, embroidery, felting—anything to do with a needle and some type of fiber. Her work can be found on her Etsy site, www.fibergarden.etsy.com.

Alice Bernardo is an architect working and living in Guimarães, Portugal. She started sewing after her daughter was born and loves anything that involves a needle and thread, or a hammer and nails. You can see more of her designs, as well as visit her shop, at www. noussnouss.com.

Margaret Couch Cogswell has been making books for more than 12 years. Although she's journeyed from weaving to ceramics, fabric collage, and now books, many of the themes and materials have stayed the same. She received her Bachelor of Arts from Rhodes College and has continued her education at Rhode Island School of Design, Arrowmont School of Arts and Crafts, and Penland School of Crafts, where she's currently a resident artist. You can contact her at mccogswell@charter.net.

Casey Dwyer has spent the past two years developing a line of felt accessories that are currently being sold worldwide. She started her business, The Candy Thief, in early 2006 with the hope of making just a bit of extra pocket change, but before long her crafting endeavor became a full-time job. Casey lives with a funky feline named Ira, and works from her upstate New York studio. Visit her shop at www.thecandythief.etsy.com.

Lindy Emser has had a long love affair with fabric and fibers and has been a maker of things from a young age, designing everything from furniture for her dollhouse to handmade beads and jewelry. While still in high school, she was designing screen-printed graphics at RISD. This led to studies at Columbia College Chicago, where a focus in printmaking encouraged her to examine urban patterns, textures, and surfaces. Chicago provided a great backdrop for finding new connections between unlikely materials: where some saw the cracks in the sidewalk, Lindy saw cross-stitch patterns. While others perceived manhole covers, Lindy imagined crocheted patches. When a favorite sweater accidentally shrunk in the wash, Lindy spotted raw material for a new project.

Lindy is the creator of PlyTextiles, a line of items for the home that puts a modern eco-spin on traditional processes for creating warmth in the home. You can find her shop at plytextiles.etsy.com.

Tamara Erbacher is a self-taught crafter whose indulgences include sewing, embroidery, knitting, crochet, printmaking, and quilting. She has a particular love of fabric, and the color and designs that come with it. She lives in Melbourne, Australia, with her husband and four boys. You can follow Tamara's crafty life at www.quarterofaninch.blogspot.com.

Rachel Fields was born and raised in the cool mountain town of Asheville, North Carolina. She now resides in the arid climate of Austin, Texas, where she's currently in the throes of pulling together a topnotch portfolio for design school.

Cheyenne Goh has been making things since the age of six. She's traveled extensively throughout the world, working on projects centered on alleviating poverty through crafting. She enjoys dreaming up new ways of recycling clothes and other bits and bobs into things of fun and function. Check out Cheyenne's recycled creations at www.RumahKampung.etsy.com.

Rachel Hayes has been sewing and making things for as long as she can remember and enjoys recycling older fabrics and garments into something new and usable. She lives in Canberra, Australia, with a loving husband, her two beautiful daughters, and four brown chooks (for non-Aussies, that means chickens!). Drop by www.lulli.etsy.com to check out her creations.

Sarah Lalone began sewing when she realized there was a need for useful everyday items that also looked good. When, in 2007, she decided it was time to share those creations, she created Punchanella. Her blog and shop can be seen at www.punchanella.com. Sarah lives and works as a student and independent designer in Ontario, Canada, with her husband and son.

Rebeka Lambert is a self-proclaimed fabric addict living on the outskirts of Baton Rouge, Louisiana, with her husband and three young children. Her love of sewing began as a child when she would watch her mother and grandmother sew, but it was the discovery of craft blogs that led her back to crafting. She has contributed to the Lark books *Pretty Little Patchwork* (2008), *Pretty Little Potholders* (2008), and *Pretty Little Purses and Pouches* (2008). You can catch a glimpse of Rebeka's life on her blog, www.artsycraftybabe.typepad.com, or at her Etsy shop, www.artsycraftybabe.etsy.com, where she periodically sells her creations.

When **Mari Livie** isn't busy creating, she can be found hunting through used clothing stores and friends' closets for unusual fabrics. She received her degree in environmental studies and ceramics at the University of Oregon. Although Mari still creates with clay, she's discovered in cloth a way to reconcile her respect for the wild, untouched places on earth with her own need to create. You can find her work at tonguetied.etsy.com or marilivie.blogspot.com.

Lisa Macchia is inspired by daydreams and fairy tales and loves to incorporate different materials and techniques into her work. She's the designer and owner of Ity-Bity Bags, where she brings playfulness and color to everyday accessories. Visit her shop at www.itybity-bags.etsy.com.

Joan K. Morris's artistic endeavors have led her down many successful creative paths, including costume design for motion pictures, and ceramics. Joan has contributed projects to numerous Lark books, including *50 Nifty Beaded Cards* (2008), *Button! Button!* (2008), *Pretty Little Potholders* (2008), *Cutting-Edge Decoupage* (2007), *Extreme Office Crafts* (2007), *Pretty Little Pincushions* (2007), and many, many more.

Stacey Murray comes from a long line of knitters and began her craft experimenting with beanies and scarves. When not knitting, blogging, sweeping the floor, or picking up toys, Stacey enjoys sewing little bits and pieces such as tea cozies, handkerchief pouches, and lipstick cozies. For more information, visit www.sheepsclothing.com.au and www.sheepsclothing.blogspot.com.

Old memories inspire many of **Dorie Blaisdell Schwarz's** designs, whether they're created on a sewing machine, with knitting needles, as a screen print, or with hot-glue gun in hand. She currently lives in Farmer City, Illinois, with her husband and their young daughter. When she's not sewing or crafting, she builds websites and renovates her Victorian-era farmhouse. Pay her a visit at tumblingblocks.net.

Jessie Senese loves to sew. She also loves thrift stores, old maps, children's books, flea markets, mod wallpaper, polka dots, costume jewelry, embroidery patterns, chocolate pudding, vintage fabric, and her darling family. Jessie stitches to her heart's content in a home studio just outside of Chicago, Illinois, and invites you to follow her misadventures in craft at www.sweetjessie.com.

Valerie Shrader made a pair of pink culottes when she was 11 and has loved fabric (and sewing) ever since. She's on the staff of Lark Books, and has written and edited many books related to textiles and needlework. Valerie knits every now and then, too, and dreams about dyeing fabric and making artful quilts when she's not watching birds.

Ruth Singer is a British textile designer who creates bespoke and limited edition textiles and accessories using organic and vintage fabrics. She's a skilled textile historian and uses traditional hand-sewing techniques such as pleating, quilting, and appliqué to create unusual textures and sculptural effects. Her work has appeared in publications including *Elle Decoration* and *The Guardian*. You can find out more on her website, www.ruthsinger.com.

Acknowledgments

First and foremost, a big round of applause to the talented designers who contributed the terrific projects in these pages. This book wouldn't, nay, *couldn't* exist without their willingness to share their flair.

Photographer Sandra Stambaugh pulled out all the stops when she styled and shot the projects; her perfect touch shows the projects to their best advantage and got the fabrics to shine in the spotlight. Art director Kristi Pfeffer was a wonderful collaborator. Although her layouts seem effortless, all kinds of gears are clicking and whirring beneath the surface. Thanks to Bradley Norris for his tireless art production assistance. Much appreciation to Magnolia Beauregard's—an antiques store in downtown Asheville, North Carolina, filled with the most wondrous items—for its generous loan of props. And let's not forget the models, including Bella the cat, who worked it hard to lend even more appeal to the photos.

Gushing thanks to the people who made sure all the i's got dotted and the t's, crossed: editorial assistant and right-hand woman Kathleen McCafferty; technical editor Beth Baumgartel; editorial interns Jacob Biba and Hannah Harrison; and proofreader Karen Levy.

About the Author

Nathalie Mornu works as an editor at Lark Books. She's dabbled in many crafts over the years, and as a sideline sometimes creates projects for Lark publications—stuff as varied as stitched potholders, beaded jewelry, an upholstered mid-century chair, a strange scarecrow made from cutlery, and a gingerbread igloo. She's the author of *A Is for Apron* (2008) and *Cutting-Edge Decoupage* (2007), and is currently producing a book of leather jewelry for release in 2010.

Index